WORD OF MOUTH

From Elaine Wells - 1997

A COLLECTION OF RECIPES FROM THE FRIENDS OF THE HUMANE SOCIETY of KNOX COUNTY ·ROCKLAND, MAINE·

COVER AND ILLUSTRATIONS

by

HOLLY BERRY

WORD OF MOUTH

All of the profits realized from WORD OF MOUTH will be used to support the homeless animals at the Humane Society of Knox County – their food, shelter, medical care and comfort. The Humane Society of Knox County hopes that readers of WORD OF MOUTH will be inspired to help their local animal shelters in one of the many ways open to them.

For additional copies, use the form at the back of the book, or send a check for $14.95 plus $2.50 shipping/handling to: WORD OF MOUTH, Box 21, Tenants Harbor, ME., 04860

ISBN: 0-9649385-0-2

Printed in the USA by

WIMMER
The Wimmer Companies, Inc.
Memphis

Dedicated to:

Two-legged Hasp

Three-legged Rocky

Four-legged Stuart

and

Winged Warren

ACKNOWLEDGMENTS

The Humane Society of Knox County is most grateful to the following friends for their generous contributions to WORD OF MOUTH. We regret that because of similarity or space considerations we were unable to include all recipes submitted.

Susie Axworthy
Jim Balano
Ruth Barnes
Ricardo Barreto
Betsy Bates
Ann Beck
Donna Bergen
Mary Jane Bergren
Judy Botsford
Heather Boyd
Janie Bracey
Deb Brickman
Paul Brodeur
Rosalind Brown
True Burley
Joan Caldwell
Nancie Chamberlain
William Chapman
Kathy Chase
Laurette Chilles
Mrs. Herbert Conway
Day Cowperthwaite
Scott Creighton
Shari Dalsheim
Bob Davis
Kay Dodge
Susan Dooley
Morris Dorenfeld
Stacey Dunphy
Harry Durt
Jill Elisofon
Marilyn Ellis
Didi Emmons
Eloise Ensor
Joyce Franklin
Michael Gee
Lou Grant
Nancy Hamilton
Janet Hanrahan
Erica Harriman
Caroline Harris
Lissa Hastings
Hope Hatch
Corinne Heautot
Jane Hennings

Linda Hicks
Vinnie Hicks
Denise Hopkins
Ursula Horsford
Trish Inman
Burleigh Jaquinto
Maureen Johnson
Aniece Kerr
Jack Lake
Myrna Levine
Patsy Lewis
Jane Lucas
Iole Magri
Barbara Mann
Nancy Martland
Anne Maxfield
Richard Maxfield
Warren Maxfield
Charles McCarthy
Ann McGuire
Anne Mortimer-Maddox
Edna Moy
Nancy O'Keefe
Margaret O'Leary
Frances Pusch
Helen Rayer
Laurel Reed
Jasper Reid
Vicky Remsen
Janet Running
Daniel Seigel
Jane Siegel
Joyce Smith
Janet Sullivan
Peter Taylor
Dorothy Tolman
Christine Urick
Ingrid Van Steenberg
Millicent Vetterlein
Varieties Video
Tracy Wells
Jean Wetherbee
Edith Williams
Virginia Williams
Sandy Yakovenko

TABLE OF CONTENTS

INTRODUCTION

We love food, and when there's time, we love to cook. We all have friends who bring us new ideas or who – with a wonderful meal – remind us of old treasures, and the many friends of the Humane Society of Knox County, food lovers and animal lovers alike, are no different. WORD OF MOUTH is our chance to share some of our favorites with you.

Because we assume that you already know how to cook, we have not begun any of the recipes with "face the stove." Most of us have rules or habits such as "never/always peel tomatoes" – fine. And of course health is a major concern these days, so when we tell you to butter a pan we're aware that you may prefer canola oil, a flavored cooking spray, or olive oil. We've used egg substitutes a lot and they really work – even in omelets, much to our delight. Cream? Cheeses? Whatever your heart desires – or can stand; low-fat or no-fat substitutes are everywhere now. Sautéing in broth offers even more possibilities – a spectrum from beef to wine, with beer, clam, fruit juice, tea and vegetable in between. (Some of the vegetarian versions are terrific – check them out at your co-op or health-food store.)

However, there are some ingredients that, luckily, do not threaten our health but do enhance the quality of our lives. We have discovered, for instance, that the best balsamic vinegar and olive oil one can afford are definitely worth trying, at least once. And that pepper tastes much better when it's freshly ground. (Some people have two grinders – a fine and a coarse one!) And packaged lemon juice is such that we always try to use fresh lemons – even if we sometimes have to substitute limes. Garlic, that magic healer, is inexpensive and easy to keep and, raw or cooked (try Garlic Confit Bob Davis), it can do amazing things for just about any dish before dessert. We've also found that it is very comforting to have a chunk of real Parmesan cheese in the freezer for grating.

That's all. There may be cat hairs in the butter, and the dog may have knocked over a glass of wine with his tail, but we at the Humane Society of Knox County hope that WORD OF MOUTH will inspire you to say, "so many recipes, so little time. . ."

Joan Maxfield, Editor

APPETIZERS

10 Accelerated Appetizers

1   A large block of cream cheese with one of the following on top: hot pepper jelly, chopped marinated artichoke hearts, or Auntie Ruth's Way Hot Chili Sauce.

2   The ultimate artery clogger, Genoa cigarettes: thinnest slices of Genoa salami spread with cream cheese and rolled up.

3   Cream cheese processed with Spanish olives and salsa or minced canned jalapeño peppers. This one we guarantee.

4   ¼" slices of cucumber with a dab of mayonnaise, a shrimp and a sprig of fresh dill or 3 beads of salmon roe as a garnish.

5   Cauliflower florets or leftover mussel meats served with a sour cream-mayonnaise sauce flavored with lemon juice and curry.

6   Stuffed grape leaves from the supermarket salad bar, cut in half, sprinkled with olive oil, salt, and lemon juice, speared with toothpicks and garnished with lemon wedges.

7   Large flour tortillas, spread with processed canned shrimp, lemon juice and mayo – or with leftover Port Clyde Crabmeat Spread Balano, or Wicked Good Artichoke Dip/Spread – rolled and cut into ½" slices. Fasten with toothpicks if necessary.

8   Mushroom caps, each stuffed with a smoked mussel, quickly popped under the broiler.

9   English muffins or split pita breads spread with any pesto and put in the toaster oven, then cut into wedges or quarters.

10 A small bowl, or round loaf of bread hollowed out, filled with any pesto and placed in the middle of a platter containing a selection of fresh veggies for dipping.

SMOKED TROUT PÂTÉ ST. GEORGE

1 smoked trout, skinned, boned, head and tail off

8 oz. cream cheese

1 T. lemon juice

1 T. cognac

½ tsp. Worcestershire sauce

salt and pepper to taste

Combine all the ingredients in a processer or blender, purée, and pack the pâté into a small crock. Serve it with melba toast or baguette rounds. (Try a portion of it, thinned with lemon juice and mayonnaise, as a dressing for new potatoes in a salad.) It will keep in the refrigerator for 4-5 days and it freezes well. Makes 1½ cups.

You can use any smoked trout for this recipe – most supermarkets carry them now – but Kohn's Smokehouse is not far from the Knox County Humane Society, and their trout is boneless; be sure to look for bones if yours comes from a supermarket. Kohn's also has, among other things, smoked monkfish tail and smoked mussels, both of which are terrific on a salad, with spaghetti, or on top of a pizza.

When training a dog, use three voice levels: a high pitched one for praising and the baby talk one uses with animals; a normal and authoritative one for commands; and a low, quick, controlled voice when making corrections. (This is the way the trainers of drug-sniffing dogs do it.)

PORT CLYDE CRABMEAT SPREAD BALANO

8 oz. fresh crabmeat

8 oz. cream cheese

2 - 4 T. mayonnaise

2 dashes Tabasco sauce

a splash of lemon juice

salt and pepper to taste

optional: dill

Preheat the oven to 375. Mix all the ingredients together and bake for 20-30 minutes until bubbly. Serve this warm with crackers and let guests spread their own. It can also be spread, unbaked, on toast points, and popped under the broiler. Serves 6-8

BROILED BREAD WITH ANCHOVIES

thick slices of dense peasant bread, broiled, grilled, or toasted

good olive oil

garlic cloves, cut in half

ripe tomatoes, cut in half

anchovy fillets

Rub the broiled bread with the garlic cloves, drizzle it with the olive oil, and rub it with the tomato halves so that the seeds and juices are soaked into each slice. Place 2 anchovy fillets on each slice and serve at once.

Why is the cat always on the wrong side of the door?

SEVICHE: SHRIMP OR SCALLOP

1 lb. fresh shrimp or scallops

½ cup fresh lime juice

2 T. olive oil

½ red bell pepper, seeded and diced fine

½ fresh jalapeño pepper, minced, or ¼ tsp. hot pepper flakes

¼ cup chopped red onion, scallion, or shallot

1 T. fresh cilantro, chopped

optional: 1 clove garlic, minced

salt and pepper to taste

Rinse and drain the scallops and cut them into quarters if large; peel and clean the shrimp. Place them in a large glass dish with all the other ingredients, blending everything well. Refrigerate for 4-6 hours before serving. (If the weather turns cold suddenly, or if you have leftovers, drain the seafood, quickly sauté it in hot olive oil, and serve it over hot pasta.) Serves 6.

MARCIE'S SHRIMPS

1½ lb. shrimp, not peeled

1 stick celery

1 carrot

2 T. wine vinegar

½ cup olive oil

¼ cup lemon juice

salt and pepper to taste

Boil the shrimps for 1 minute in 2 quarts of water with the celery, carrot, and vinegar. Remove them at once, peel them while still warm, and marinate them for 1 hour at room temperature in the oil, juice, salt and pepper. If you are not ready to serve them, chill them until you are, and serve at room temperature.

TARAMASALATA

4 slices white bread, crusts removed

3 T. tarama (carp roe – Middle Eastern grocery store)

2 T. lemon juice

¾ cup olive oil

Soak the bread in cold water and squeeze it dry. Using an electric beater, briefly combine the tarama and the lemon juice in a bowl. Add the bread, a little at a time, and beat it in. Then add the olive oil in a slow stream – the result will resemble mayonnaise. Serve this with pita bread or sesame crackers. Serves 4-6.

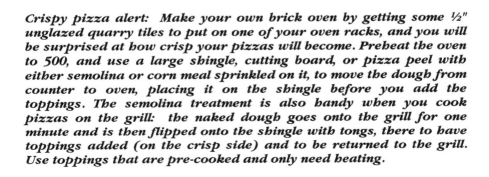

Crispy pizza alert: Make your own brick oven by getting some ½" unglazed quarry tiles to put on one of your oven racks, and you will be surprised at how crisp your pizzas will become. Preheat the oven to 500, and use a large shingle, cutting board, or pizza peel with either semolina or corn meal sprinkled on it, to move the dough from counter to oven, placing it on the shingle before you add the toppings. The semolina treatment is also handy when you cook pizzas on the grill: the naked dough goes onto the grill for one minute and is then flipped onto the shingle with tongs, there to have toppings added (on the crisp side) and to be returned to the grill. Use toppings that are pre-cooked and only need heating.

8 oz. package phyllo dough

¾ cup unsalted butter, melted

½ lb. fresh asparagus, cut into 1" pieces

¼ lb. feta cheese, crumbled

½ cup yogurt

2 eggs, beaten

3 scallions, chopped

Preheat the oven to 375. Brush the thawed phyllo dough with the melted butter, and cut it into 4" squares. Layer three squares at a time, each one turned slightly, to make a frilled edge, and carefully push them into buttered muffin tins. Keep them covered while preparing the filling; that is, mixing all the other ingredients in a bowl. Fill each cup to within ½" of the top and bake about 25 minutes – until the pastry is crisp and golden and the filling is set and risen. Allow to cool for about 10 minutes before serving. Serves 6-8.

This wonderful brunch/lunch can be served cold, and you may substitute spinach, fresh or frozen-and-squeezed-out, for the asparagus. If so, you might sauté it quickly first in real butter with a little lemon juice and a pinch of nutmeg, before chopping it for the filling.

If you're using phyllo dough for the first time, fear not; simply follow the package instructions carefully for slow thawing. Remember to keep the dough covered with a dampened towel as soon as you unwrap it and stack it. When you brush it, keep your strokes light, and move the brush from the middle towards the edges; this prevents tearing. If it tears, stay cool; patching is permitted, and doesn't show. As soon as you discover what fun, how easy, and how rewarding working with phyllo dough is, you'll be wrapping everything in it but the cat.

FETA PITA BREAD & RUFFLED GRAPE LEAVES

½ lb. feta cheese

2 T. olive oil

1 T. lemon juice, or to taste

small pita breads, split, or 6" tortillas

fresh parsley, dried oregano, or toasted pine nuts, for garnish

1 egg

Mash and mix the first 3 ingredients, spread them on the pita breads, garnish, and toast under a broiler or in a toaster oven. Cut them into wedges and serve. To make ruffled grape leaves, add an egg to the mixture above, and preheat the oven to 350. Oil a quart oven-proof serving dish, and line it completely with grape leaves – from a jar, or fresh – rough side down, which you have drained, dried and oiled (or sprayed) on the smooth side, leaving a ruffled collar sticking up. Put the cheese mixture into the dish, and bake it at 350 until the cheese is soft and the ruffles a bit dry – 10 to 15 minutes. Garnish, and serve it with fresh vegetables to dip, or the usual suspects: crusty bread slices and white wine. Serves 4.

One of a friend's favorite summertime grilling activities consists of rolling up oily sun-dried tomatoes with chunks of goat cheese in grape leaves, securing them with wet toothpicks, and grilling them for a minute on each side – great with slices of baguette. Another filling is small pieces of feta cheese. (If you pick your own leaves, simply pour boiling water over them before you use them.)

WICKED GOOD ARTICHOKE DIP/SPREAD

1 cup stuffing mix

1 cup warm milk or broth

¾ lb. artichoke hearts in oil

1 small onion, chopped

1 clove garlic, chopped

2 eggs, lightly beaten

¼ tsp. dried basil or oregano

½ tsp. Tabasco or 1 tsp. hot sauce

8 oz. mild cheese, shredded

4 T. fresh parsley, chopped

salt and pepper to taste

Soak the stuffing mix in the milk or broth while you prepare the rest of the dish. Drain the oil (you will need about 2 T.) from the artichokes into a 2-quart baking dish; add the onion and garlic, cover with wax paper, and microwave on HIGH for 3 minutes, stirring once, until the onion is soft. Chop the artichokes, and put them into a bowl with the rest of the ingredients, including the stuffing; add this to the onion mix so that all is blended in the baking dish. Cover it with wax paper and microwave on HIGH for 10 minutes, turning at least once during cooking, until it's set. Leave the dish covered for 10 more minutes on a counter surface, not a wire rack, to finish "cooking". Makes 4 cups.

This dish can be served warm or cold, as a dip or as a spread. It's good on toast points with a fast finish under the broiler. If you wish to make it in a conventional oven, preheat it to 350. Sauté the onion and the garlic and then combine all the ingredients in an oven-proof dish, and bake for 45 minutes.

The cat has too much spirit to have no heart. Ernest Menault

CARIOCA CARROT DIP

3 carrots, peeled and cut into small pieces
6 T. water
pinch sugar
1 T. olive oil
2 T. vinegar
¼ tsp. salt
1 small clove garlic, minced

Cook the carrots in the water with the sugar until they're soft, about 5 minutes. Drain all but 1 T. of the water (saving the rest in case you need to add it later) and put it and the carrots into a blender or processer with the rest of the ingredients. Blend and, if too thick (it should have the consistency of sour cream), add liquid. Use this as a dip for vegetables, especially mushrooms, florets of cauliflower, cucumber, and yes, even carrot sticks. Makes a scant cup.

When a friend had this quirky sauce at a Brazilian restaurant as an appetizer with fried yucca, he begged for the recipe, and was given only a list of the odd ingredients and a small sample to take home. (He spilled half of it on the way!) After trying several combinations of the ingredients, he came up with an exact replica. It's so quick to make, he serves it often – even kids love it.

Dogs see humans as members of the pack – cats do not: with their solitary heritage, cats see humans as Mother substitutes.

SUSIE AND JANET'S CAVIAR DIP

1 pint sour cream

8 oz. cream cheese

1 bunch scallions, green part only, chopped fine

1 small jar (2-4 oz.) caviar, red or black

Combine all but the caviar in a processer or blender. Pour it into a serving dish and spread the caviar on top. Serve this with ripple potato chips or perhaps with something very chic, like little crustless toast points. This is always the first thing to disappear at parties. Makes 3 cups.

CROCKED OLIVES

Buy an assortment of your favorite olives-in-a-barrel: black, green, and brown, large and small. Take them home and put them in a nice clear glass jar, and fill it with your best olive oil, bay leaves, slivers of lemon peel, pepper corns, toasted pine nuts, sprigs of rosemary, etc. and leave them for a few days. When you need a quick appetizer, serve them in small bowls, oil included (for dipping the crusty bread which will accompany them), with lots of bright paper napkins and glasses of wine. It's instant gracious living, and the jar is everlasting: just be sure the olives have their heads under oil, and replenish them as you need.

If called by a panther, don't anther. Ogden Nash

RUSTY ROASTED RED PEPPER DIP

6 red bell peppers, washed, quartered, and seeded

2 T. olive oil

1 onion, sliced thin

1 jalapeño or small hot pepper, seeded and minced

2 large cloves garlic, chopped fine

5 tsp. ground cumin

½ cup fresh parsley, chopped

juice and pulp of 2 limes

3 T. dark brown sugar

salt and pepper to taste

Turn on the broiler and preheat it while you prepare the peppers for roasting, and arrange them on a baking sheet, skin side up. Broil them for about 10 minutes, rearranging them as necessary, until the skins are mostly blackened. Put them into a brown paper bag or a covered bowl to steam for 5 minutes before peeling; their skins will slip right off. Meanwhile, heat the oil and sauté the onion in a skillet for 5-10 minutes, until soft and translucent. Add the next 3 ingredients and cook, stirring, for another minute. (You can buy cumin in seed form and toast it in a heated frying pan, shaking or stirring it, for a few minutes. When you grind it, the flavor will astonish you.) Cut the peppers into smaller pieces and then puree them with all the other ingredients; use whatever method you like, tasting for seasoning before serving, and adding more oil if necessary. Makes about 2 cups.

Forgive the wordy directions; the dish takes less time to make than to read about! This makes a great dip for vegetables, toast points, melba rounds, or pita bread. It is also terrific for smearing on slices of broiled eggplant on a pizza, including the English muffin or split pita bread ones you can make in the toaster oven. You might also like to use it as one more version of red pesto. Or add 2 cups of broth and 1 of yogurt, sour cream, or buttermilk for a smooth and quirky summer soup.

great make 1/2

BOOK CLUB GUACAMOLE SALSA DIP FOR A CROWD

3 cups onions, chopped
3 cups tomatoes, peeled and chopped
2 avocados (not too soft), peeled, seeded, and chopped
juice of 2 limes
2 cloves garlic, minced
1 tiny can serrano chilis, finely chopped
3 T. fresh cilantro, chopped
salt and pepper to taste

Everything should be chopped by hand, not in a blender or processer, because what we want here is texture to complement the fabulous flavors. Mix gently and serve as a dip with taco chips. Makes 6 cups.

Perhaps because of its texture, this dip was an instant hit when it was served at the book club's "The Wild Sargasso Sea" meeting. The readers agreed that for once guacamole was not an innocuous puddle, and they plotted various ways to use it as a salsa, too.

(One of them reminded the others that when the classic puddle was called for, to be sure to save the avocado pit, rinse it and use it as a center garnish, to prevent discoloration.)

It was Vixen's custom . . . to sleep in my bed, her head on the pillow like a Christian; and when morning came I would always find that the little thing had braced her feet against the wall and pushed me to the very edge of the cot. Rudyard Kipling

MARINATED HERB GARDEN CHEESE COINS

2 4-oz. logs goat cheese, or any other soft cheese

½ cup olive oil

2 cloves garlic, sliced

8 peppercorns, crushed (use bottom of frying pan)

1 generous sprig fresh rosemary, or 4 of fresh thyme, crushed

2 bay leaves, broken up

optional: strips of lemon peel

Cut the rounds of cheese into ½" thick coins, and put them in a small glass or porcelain dish just large enough to hold them. Heat the oil with the next 4 or 5 ingredients until it's very hot, pour all of it over the cheese, and let it cool to room temperature. Refrigerate the dish, covered, for a few hours and serve the rounds in their dish at room temperature accompanied by slices of baguette. Serves 4-8.

This works with yogurt cheese (you'll have a larger round, for a group instead of individuals) and baby mozzarellas, and even good old Neufchatel. You can vary the marinade, including basil, sage, hot pepper flakes, etc., and even garnish with pink peppercorns, although these coins are fetching enough in their green and yellow garb. It's fun to have a lot of them refrigerated in a pretty jar for last minute appetizers, and the marinade can be renewed, reused and refilled ad infinitum.

A sleeping cat is ever alert. Fred Schwab

DISAPPEARING CHEESE TRUFFLES

12 oz. brie, trimmed and softened

4 oz. cream cheese

1 stick (8 T.) sweet butter

2 T. cognac

4-6 drops hot pepper sauce

salt and pepper to taste

2 cups fine bread crumbs: black bread, for instance

In a processer or mixing machine, combine all but the bread, and mix until smooth. Refrigerate overnight. (It will last for at least three days, if you wish to make it ahead.) Form the cheese mix into 1" balls and roll them in the bread crumbs so that they are completely covered. Refrigerate, covered, before serving. Makes about 48.

The feline ten-second energy-saving rule: If it takes more than ten seconds in an open door for your cat to decide whether it wants to go out, close the door.

BALL OF BREAD WITH BRIE

4 cloves garlic, minced

4 scallions, chopped fine

8 oz. cream cheese, cut into pieces, room temperature

8 oz. brie with rind removed, cut into pieces, room temperature

6 oz. sour cream

1 T. lemon or lime juice

1 tsp. Worcestershire sauce

2 tsp. brown sugar

salt and pepper to taste

optional: 2 T. cognac

1 18-oz. round loaf of bread: pumpernickel, sourdough, etc.

raw vegetables to serve with the bread

Preheat the oven to 400. Combine everything but the bread in a processer, and season it with salt and pepper. Cut off the top of the loaf and scoop out the center, leaving a ¾" shell. Put the cheese mix in, replace the lid and wrap the loaf in foil. (It can be prepared a day ahead and refrigerated. Let it stand at room temperature an hour before baking.) Bake the ball for 30-45 minutes, and then unwrap it, remove the lid, and continue baking until it bubbles. Place it on a serving dish with the top removed, sprinkle the cheese with paprika, and serve it with the vegetables around it – some choices might be tiny asparagus spears, strips of any color bell pepper, mushrooms, or cauliflower florets. Serves 6-10.

If man could be crossed with a cat it would improve man, but it would deteriorate the cat. Mark Twain

1 10-oz. pkg. frozen bake-and-fill pastry shells, thawed
½ cup pesto pomodoro (see sauces), or your current favorite
½ cup broccoli stems, sliced tomatoes, or black olives, chopped
1/3 cup shredded cheese: pepper jack, smoked mozzarella, etc.
olive oil, garlic slivers, and salt and pepper for sprinkling
optional: fresh parsley or basil for garnish

Roll out the pastry shells on a floured board to about 6". Preheat the oven to 375. If you are using the broccoli stems, peel and julienne them and steam or blanch them for a few minutes until they are barely tender. Spread a thin layer of the pesto on each tart shell, top it with the stems, drizzle with oil, sprinkle with a bit of cheese and salt and pepper, and bake on an ungreased cookie sheet for 20 minutes, or until browned. Cut them into quarters for appetizers – for a snack or first course, serve them whole. Makes 6.

We are leaving the toppings a bit vague, because these are such fun to make. Green pesto with sliced tomatoes and black olives, for instance; cheese or no cheese, garlic or basil, etc.; it's fun to make up combinations. Walnut pesto and parsley, for example, with maybe toasted pine nuts on top – just empty the fridge and have at it.

No animal admires another animal. Pascal

CHEESE AND PEPPER STICKS

2/3 cup Parmesan cheese

1 T. cracked pepper, large grind

2 cups flour

1 T. baking powder

½ tsp. baking soda

¼ tsp. salt

3 T. butter, very cold, cut into pieces

1 cup buttermilk

2 T. melted butter for brushing on before baking

Preheat the oven to 450. Use a non-stick baking sheet, or line one with parchment paper. Put the cheese and black pepper in a blender or processer, and mix quickly. Add the dry ingredients, and combine by turning the machine on and off several times. Add the butter to the processer, pulsing on and off several times, until the dough becomes grainy. Pour in the buttermilk with the machine running and blend, until the dough just starts to stay together. Do not let it form a ball. Flour your hands and gather the dough together into a ball, kneading it on a lightly floured surface until barely smooth, no more than ten times. With a floured rolling pin, roll it out into a 9x12" rectangle. With a very sharp knife, cut it into sticks 1½" x 3". Use all the dough, including the scraps. Place them on the baking sheet at least an inch apart, brush them with the melted butter, and bake them for about 10 minutes, until golden. (If you are allowed salt, you might think about sprinkling the tops with the coarse stuff before baking. If not, consider reserving 1 teaspoon of the pepper for that purpose.) Makes 2 dozen.

To entice a cat to use a scratching post, rub catnip on it.

BLUE CHEESE COOKIES

2¼ cups sifted flour

½ tsp. salt

½ tsp. white pepper

½ cup powdered sugar

8 oz. butter

1 cup blue cheese, crumbled

3 T. dry sherry

1½ cups walnuts, toasted and finely chopped

Sift together the dry ingredients; cut in the butter until it resembles corn meal. Add the cheese and mix with a wooden spoon. Sprinkle the sherry and 1 cup of the walnuts over the dough and mix until it's stiff. Divide it in half and form it into two rolls about 9" long and 1" in diameter. Roll them in the rest of the walnuts, pressing them into the dough. Wrap them in wax paper and chill until firm, about 1 hour. When you're ready to bake, preheat the oven to 400, cut the rolls into ¼" slices, and bake them on lightly sprayed baking sheets for about 8 minutes, or until they're golden. Cool on wire racks. Serve them with a glass of white wine, or as dessert, with fruit and cheese on the side. Makes 5 dozen.

Make boots for your dog's winter walks by using golf club covers, baby booties, or small socks. Sew vinyl or leather on the bottoms, if you have time, for double protection.

CAPRICORN CRACKERS

2/3 cup flour

3 T. sweet butter

5 oz. goat cheese, crumbled

3 T. sour cream

1 egg white, lightly beaten

coarse salt

Combine the first 4 ingredients into a soft dough in a processer (or in a bowl, cutting the butter into the flour and stirring in the cheese and the sour cream until it is blended). Roll the dough into logs about 1" in diameter. Wrap them in plastic and chill until they are firm, at least an hour. When you are ready to bake, preheat the oven to 350 and cut into coins about ¼" thick. Prick them with a fork, brush with the egg white, sprinkle with salt, and bake them for 12-15 minutes, until they are lightly browned. Cool them on wire racks, and serve with cocktails. Makes about 2 dozen.

Be sure to take the leash off your dog when it is in the car; the leash could become tangled or caught on something in the car.

SOUPS

10 Recipes in This Cookbook to Make for Your Favorite Nephew

1 Taramasalata

2 Focaccia

3 The Mayo Clinic

4 Tequila Mockingbird

5 Linen Polenta

6 Garlic Smashed Potatoes

7 Meg's Crackly Sauce for Ice Cream

8 Avocado Pear Cream

9 Tortilla Lasagne

10 Mt. Desert Dessert

CAMDEN HARBOR FISH CHOWDER

6 large potatoes, peeled or unpeeled, cubed

1 qt. chicken broth

3 1/8" slices salt pork, diced fine (or bacon)

3 large onions, rough chopped

1 green bell pepper, diced

2 large cloves garlic, slivered

¼ cup white wine

1½ - 2 lb. hake or any white fish, cut into 2" cubes

2 cups milk, more or less

salt to taste

In a large saucepan, simmer the potatoes in the broth until just barely tender, (about 10 minutes), turn off their heat and reserve, liquid and all. Meanwhile, in another large pot, render the salt pork until fat appears and the cubes become golden. Add the onions and pepper in two batches, sautéeing each one for about 5-7 minutes. The garlic goes in with the second batch, and when everything smells good and looks slightly limp, turn up the heat, add the wine, and let it reduce for a minute. Now add the potatoes and 2 cups of their broth, the fish (people choose hake for several reasons: it's delicious, it's cheap and plentiful in Maine, and it disintegrates in a nice soup-thickening way when cooked, without disappearing altogether) and 1 cup of milk. Turn down the heat and let the liquid begin to simmer, watching carefully so it does not boil. When the fish turns white, the chowder is done and you can add more milk if you like, and taste for salt. At this point, it can be refrigerated, to be served another day, or served at once with a dab of butter floating on the surface and a dash of paprika for garnish. Serves 6.

A short horse is soon curried. John Heywood

JACQUELINE KENNEDY'S NEW ENGLAND FISH CHOWDER

2 lb. fresh haddock

2 oz. salt pork, diced

2 onions, sliced

4 large potatoes, diced

1 cup celery, chopped

1 bay leaf, crumbled

1 tsp. salt

ground black pepper to taste

1 qt. milk

2 T. butter

Simmer the haddock in 2 cups of water for 15 minutes; drain and reserve the broth. Remove the bones from the fish and discard. In a heavy skillet, sauté the diced pork until it's crisp, and remove. Sauté the onions in the pork fat until they're golden brown. Add the fish, potatoes, celery, bay leaf, and salt and pepper. Pour in the fish broth plus enough boiling water to make 3 cups of liquid. Simmer for 15 minutes or until the potatoes are tender. Add the milk and heat again, topping with bits of butter when serving. Serves 6.

This recipe appeared in the early sixties in a Brookline, Massachusetts, public school fund-raiser cookbook.

Cats asleep on the shelves like motorized bookends. Audrey Thomas

ANDORRA FISH STEW

3 T. olive oil

2 large onions, sliced

4 large cloves garlic, smashed

1 28-oz. can crushed tomatoes

1 bottle dry red wine

½ cup fresh parsley, chopped, or 2 T. fresh thyme sprigs

4-6 cups leftover white-fleshed fish, in 2" lumps

salt and pepper to taste

In a large heavy pot, heat the oil and quickly sauté the onions and garlic until soft. Add the tomatoes and bring to a boil, then the wine and the parsley, ditto. Simmer for about 15 minutes, and then add the fish, warming it thoroughly and tasting for seasoning. Serve in warmed soup bowls with the requisite salad, bread, and wine. Serves 6-8.

The original fish used in this stew was grilled – a typical method of cooking fish in Spain. If you do grill fish, think about buying an extra hunk for this divine stew.

When your dog misbehaves, say "No" in a loud, quick, firm voice. As soon as it obeys, shower it with praise, rewards, and affection.

PICK OF THE LITTER LOBSTER BISQUE

shells and cut-up meat from 2 small cooked lobsters

1 cup milk

2 T. butter

2 T. flour

1 cup half-and-half or light cream

2 T. tomato juice or 1 tsp. tomato paste

½ tsp. ground mace

¼ cup sherry

salt and pepper to taste

Crush the shells and simmer them for 15 minutes in the milk. Pour it through a fine sieve, pressing the shells to remove every scrap of flavor. Meanwhile, in a skillet, heat the butter and whisk in the flour, making it into a paste. Blend in the cream, the tomato juice and the mace, and slowly whisk in the lobster-shell milk, bringing it almost to the boil. Stir the bisque as it thickens, then add the sherry and the lobster meat and simmer for exactly 1 minute. Taste for seasoning and serve at once. Serves 2-3.

A horse is dangerous at both ends and uncomfortable in the middle.
Ian Fleming

MICROWAVE ARTICHOKE AND OYSTER STEW
BOURBON STREET

1 small onion, minced

2 T. butter

2 T. flour

1 cup bottled clam juice or strong chicken broth

1 can (14-16 oz.) artichoke hearts, drained and rough chopped, or

  1 pkg. (10 oz.) frozen artichoke hearts, thawed and rough chopped

1 cup light cream

1 cup (8 oz.) shucked oysters and their liquid

Tabasco or hot sauce to taste

salt and pepper to taste

fresh chopped parsley and/or lemon zest strings for garnish

Place the onion and the butter in a 3-quart, casserole, cover it with wax paper, and microwave on HIGH for 2 minutes, or until the onion is tender. Whisk in the flour to blend and then mix in the broth and the artichokes. Cover, and microwave for 3 minutes or until bubbling. Add the cream and the oysters with their liquid, and cook for another 5 minutes, or until the oysters curl around the edges. Taste for seasoning after adding the hot sauce and the salt and pepper, ladle the stew into warm plates, garnish, and serve. Serves 4.

Sock it to your sprains and pains, aches and arthritis: pour a pound of rice into a sock and fasten it with a rubber band. Place it upside down in another sock for a double seal, again securing it with a rubber band, and put the remedy into a microwave oven on HIGH for 1-2 minutes. Drape it around the pain and relax while you watch the evening news.

ARMENIAN LEMON AND MEATBALL SOUP

¾ lb. ground raw lamb
¼ cup raw rice
1 small onion, finely chopped
2 T. parsley, finely chopped
salt and pepper to taste
optional: ½ tsp. allspice
2 quarts rich chicken broth
3 eggs
juice of 2 lemons

Combine the lamb, rice, onion, parsley, and seasonings and shape the mixture into small balls. In a large pot, bring the chicken broth to a boil, turn down the heat and add the meatballs. Simmer them, covered, for 20 minutes, until they are cooked. Remove the meatballs with a slotted spoon to a warmed bowl and reserve. Beat the eggs together with the lemon juice until they are frothy, then carefully beat in ½ cup of the broth. Add another ½ cup and pour the mixture slowly into the soup pot, stirring constantly. Do not boil. Add the meatballs, heat, and serve, dressed with parsley. Serves 6-8.

If a cat lets his tongue hang out, he's relaxed. If he licks his lips, he's anxious.

PENELOPE GILLIATT'S EASTER SUNDAY FIRST COURSE

1 can consommé madrilène soup, undiluted

8 oz. cream cheese

salt to taste

sour cream, shrimp, red caviar, and parsley for garnish

Combine the consommé and the cream cheese in a blender or processer, and taste for seasoning. Pour into small glass cups or bowls and chill. Garnish like crazy and serve as a cold soup. Serves 5-6.

(This recipe was given to Penelope Gilliatt and Mary McCarthy by Lillian Hellman during a long-ago weekend in Castine. Ms. Gilliatt once shared it with a member of the Humane Society of Knox County.)

THANKSGIVING PUMPKIN SOUP

½ cup onions, chopped

2 T. butter

1 can pumpkin pie filling

2 cans cream of chicken soup

2 soup cans (about 21 oz.) milk

sour cream and chopped, toasted hazelnuts for garnish

Sauté the onions slowly in the butter; combine them with all the other ingredients and heat, stirring. Embellish and serve. Serves 4-6.

The dog is worth its food. Greek proverb

MUSCONGUS BAY MELON SOUP

1 perfect melon (cantaloupe or honeydew), peeled and cubed

3 cups orange juice or limeade from frozen concentrate

zest of 1 and juice and pulp of 2 lemons or limes

4 T. honey or sugar

pinch of salt

1 cup nonfat lemon or vanilla yogurt

optional: 2 T. orange-flavored liqueur

fresh nasturtium blossoms or mint for garnish

Puree the melon and put it into a large bowl. Whisk in the rest of the ingredients, chill, and serve. We used orange juice and lemons with the cantaloupe; limeade (use only ¾ the amount of water called for when you reconstitute it) and limes with the honeydew. An adventurous friend used ginger ale, vanilla yogurt, and fresh grated ginger with her cantaloupe and raved about it. Serves 6-8.

To make butter for your heart, mix ½ cup canola oil, ½ lb. softened butter, and 2 T. granular lecithin (at health food stores) in a blender or processer, and store it in the refrigerator. The lecithin is supposed to reduce the butter's level of cholesterol, and the taste is — well, try it yourself, and enjoy it without guilt. We are indebted to that frugal gourmet, Jeff Smith, for this ingenious idea.

VICKY'S QUICK JELLIED BORSCHT

1 can (10 ¾ oz.) condensed beef broth

1 envelope unflavored gelatin

1 can (16 oz.) diced beets and its juice, beets chopped

1 T. horseradish, or to taste

lemon juice to taste

sour cream and snipped fresh chives for garnish

Pour ½ cup of the beef broth into a small saucepan and add the gelatin. Let it soften for 10 minutes and then slowly heat to dissolve it. Combine the minced beets in a bowl with the horseradish and all the liquids, including warm and cool beef broth and the beet juice. Check for seasoning, chill until it's jellied, and embellish before serving. Serves 4.

This soup, perfect for a summer's day, takes little time to prepare and comes out gently jellied, not firm.

Dachshunds are ideal dogs for small children, as they are already stretched and pulled to such a length that the child cannot do much harm one way or the other. Robert Benchley

GAZPACHO VERDE

6 medium yellow tomatoes, peeled

1 large cucumber, peeled and seeded; half diced, half cut up

1 large sweet onion, peeled; half diced, half cut up

1 green pepper, seeded; half diced, half cut up

1-2 cloves garlic

1 ripe avocado, peeled and diced

1/3 cup balsamic vinegar

Tabasco to taste

salt and pepper to taste

optional: fresh cilantro, chopped, and lime wedges for garnishes

All of the vegetables will be diced for adding at the last minute, and cut up into 1" chunks for pureeing. Cut 3 of the tomatoes into eighths, put them into a saucepan with ¼ cup of water and simmer them for 3-5 minutes, or until barely soft. Puree them in a blender or processer, and set the juice aside. Of the remaining 3 tomatoes, dice 2 and set them aside, and cut up the other one into chunks. Now puree all of the chunks with 1 cup of the juice and the garlic, and put the result into a large bowl. Whisk in the rest of the juice and the seasonings, and add all of the diced vegetables. To serve, place the soup in individual bowls with the diced avocado – and cilantro, if you wish, on top. Serves 6-8.

If you pick up a starving dog and make him prosperous, he will not bite you. This is the principal difference between a dog and a man.
Mark Twain

YOGURT AND CUCUMBER SOUP

1 pint yogurt

1 medium-sized cucumber, peeled, seeded, and grated

1 or 2 cloves garlic, crushed with

½ tsp. salt

2 tsp. fresh mint, finely chopped, or 1 tsp. dried mint

2 tsp. lemon juice

2 T. olive oil

pepper to taste

In a deep bowl, gently combine the yogurt with the cucumber and stir in all the other ingredients. Taste it for seasoning, adding more salt if necessary, and refrigerate for about 2 hours. Serve the soup with an ice cube in each bowl, on a hot August day. Garnish with mint. Serves 2-4.

For a thicker, larger version serving 6-8 and used as a salad, double everything, and before combining the ingredients, drain a quart of yogurt for 2-24 hours in a sieve lined with a coffee filter (drink the liquid – it's good for you). You won't need the ice cubes.

One can pick a cat to fit almost any kind of decor, color scheme, income, personality, mood. But under the fur...there still lies, essentially unchanged, one of the world's free souls. Eric Gurney

COOL CURRIED ZUCCHINI SOUP

2 lb. zucchini, thickly sliced

1 large onion, coarsely chopped

2 large cloves garlic, chopped

3 cups chicken or vegetable broth

1 tsp. curry powder

salt and pepper to taste

1 cup sour cream

½ cup fresh chives, chopped, for garnish

Put all of the ingredients but the sour cream and the chives into a large saucepan and cook on medium heat for 12 minutes. Let it cool, then put it into a blender or processer and puree. Chill; then stir in the sour cream, garnish with the chives, and serve. Serves 6.

A variation, uncurried, and without the garlic, is to sauté the onion until transparent in a small skillet while you cook the zucchini in the broth and combine the rest of the ingredients as directed above.

There are several reasons humans and dogs can communicate so comfortably. One . . . is that . . . dogs train their owners to respond to particular signals. Karol Rice

FUL MADAMMAS – AROMATIC BROWN BEANS

1 20-oz. can ful madammas (from a Near Eastern grocery)

2 large cloves garlic, crushed

3 T. fresh parsley, chopped fine

4 T. olive oil

2 lemons: juice of 1, wedges of another

½ tsp. salt

optional: 2 hard-boiled eggs and/or Greek olives for garnish

Drain and rinse the beans, and put them in a bowl with the garlic and parsley, mashing them slightly with a fork. In a separate bowl, whisk together the oil, lemon juice, and salt and stir it into the beans. Serve at room temperature in bowls, garnished, or heat and present as a soup sprinkled with parsley, drizzled with olive oil and served with lemon wedges. Serves 2-3.

A Near Eastern restaurant serves this delicious dish as an appetizer-soup. It is a national treasure, eaten for breakfast, lunch or brunch, warm or cold, with hard-boiled eggs cut up and crushed into it, with feta cheese, cucumbers, or olives, and always pita bread. Once you try it, you'll keep cans of ful madammas on hand, because it's so easy to prepare and everyone loves it.

According to a science teacher we know, it's easy to tell a hard-boiled egg from an uncooked one – simply spin them. The raw one won't budge; the hard-boiled one will become a top.

COLD BREAD SOUP

1 cup peasant bread, fresh or stale, cut in cubes, crusts removed

2 cups warm broth, vegetable or meat

3 bell peppers, any color, rough chopped

6 tomatoes, quartered

2 T. wine vinegar or lemon juice

1 tsp. sugar

½ tsp. salt

olive oil, fresh parsley, basil, or chives for garnish

shaved Parmesan cheese for garnish

Soak the bread in the broth until it's soft. Squeeze out the liquid and reserve. Put all but the garnishes into a processer, pulsing until blended. Test the soup for seasoning and chill it until you're ready to serve, at which time garnish and drizzle with olive oil. Serves 4.

You've seen that look. The way a young painter looks at a Rembrandt or Titian. The way Liz Taylor looks at Richard Burton. The way Zsa Zsa looks at mink. That's how a poodle looks at its master.
Jacqueline Susann

BLENDER VICHYSSOISE

2 medium-sized potatoes, peeled and cubed, about ½ lb.

2 onions, chopped

1 T. butter or oil

2 cups broth, or more for a thinner soup

1/8 tsp. nutmeg

salt and pepper to taste

½ cup cream, or more if desired

1 T. chives, chopped, for garnish

optional: sour cream, curry powder, for garnish

Boil the potatoes until they are tender; drain and dry. Sauté the onions in the butter for 5 minutes; add 1 cup of the broth, and simmer for 15 minutes. Place all the ingredients except the cream and garnishes in a blender or processer and puree until the soup is well blended. Chill it thoroughly. Just before serving, stir in the cream, thin to your liking with more broth if necessary, taste for seasoning, and decorate. Serves 4.

There are two means of refuge from the miseries of life; music and cats. Albert Schweitzer

BUTTERMILK COOLER WITH SHRIMP

¼-½ lb. Maine shrimp, fresh or frozen, peeled

2 strips lemon peel

1 garlic clove, crushed

2 cucumbers, peeled, seeded, and cut into chunks

1 pint buttermilk

¼ cup fresh dill, chopped

salt and pepper to taste

Steam the shrimp for a few minutes with the lemon peel and garlic until they're just barely pink; reserve. Put the remaining ingredients in a blender or processer and puree; taste for seasoning. Chop the shrimp and add them; chill and serve. Serves 4.

"Cat training" is well nigh impossible, but food bribes may work if they're offered as rewards for desired behavior.

SALADS & DRESSINGS

10 Speedy Salads

1 Thinnest slices of raw fresh scallops arranged around a pile of watercress, with red onion rings or red pepper strips and a very lemony vinaigrette.

2 Fresh spinach with a balsamic vinaigrette, blue cheese, and caramelized walnuts: place ½ cup in a skillet with 1 T. sugar and 1 T. butter; fry, stirring until crisp and shiny, 1-2 minutes.

3 Grilled shrimp on a bed of pureed watercress (sauté quickly, rinse with white wine or broth, season, and puree) garnished with chives and red pepper flakes and dressed with a lime vinaigrette.

4 Sliced fresh pears on a bed of lettuce, dressed with a lemon vinaigrette and garnished with slivered fresh ginger and toasted pecans.

5 Arugula base, tiny whole beets, red onions and oranges sliced paper thin, orange vinaigrette with zest, and toasted walnuts.

6 Cucumber slices with tons of cracked black pepper, vinegar, and chopped parsley. Optional: chopped Greek olives and/or chives.

7 Sliced green apples with toasted walnuts, balsamic vinai-grette, and shaved Parmesan on a bed of shredded red cabbage.

8 Midsummer treat: sliced yellow tomatoes with your favorite dressing, scattered with borage blossoms – worth planting the herb!

9 A can or two of white beans with any kind of pesto, thinned a bit. Add diced bell pepper of a contrasting color and/or an appropriate garnish, tuned to the pesto.

10 Crabmeat moistened with tequila on a bed of lettuce, dressed with mayonnaise mixed with drained salsa and Ta-basco. Sprinkle with fresh cilantro.

VIRGIN MARY ASPIC

2 T. unflavored gelatin (2 envelopes)
3½ cups tomato juice
½ cup ketchup
2 T. lemon juice
1 T. horseradish
few drops Tabasco

Soak the gelatin in ½ cup of the tomato juice for 10 minutes, while you combine all the other ingredients in a medium-sized saucepan. Heat this mixture slowly until it is very warm but not hot, and then add the gelatin mixture and stir until dissolved. Pour the aspic into a 4-cup ring mold and chill until firm. Unmold it and serve it with a dressing of 1 cup sour cream, ¼ cup mayonnaise, and 2 T. lemon juice. (A very festive dish might include a crabmeat center. Simply mix an 8-oz. carton of fresh or a 6-oz. can of crabmeat with about ½ cup of mayonnaise, 2 T. chili sauce, and 2 T. lemon juice. Pile it in the center of the mold, and wait for compliments.) Serves 6-8.

We love this dish so much that we have devised a method of using a large (46-oz.) can of tomato juice: you will multiply everything by 1½, i.e., 3 envelopes of gelatin soaked in ¾ cup of juice, etc., which means pouring yourself ½ cup of juice and drinking it. No need to measure the part you heat: just pour the rest of the can into the pan! Use two 3-cup molds, or that beautiful big lobster one your sister gave you.

When all candles be out, all cats be grey. John Heywood

PEMAQUID POINT CHICK PEA SALAD

1 19-oz. can chick peas
¼ cup parsley, finely chopped
½ tsp. garlic, finely chopped
3 T. lemon juice
2 T. olive oil
salt and pepper to taste

Combine all the ingredients and taste for seasoning. Serves 3-4.

This salad is perfect for a picnic, especially if it's garnished with wedges of tomato, slices of cucumber, and Greek olives. It's easy to double or triple for a crowd.

In all dog training, use praise to replace food as soon as you can, because a dog trained with only food tends to concentrate on it, and not on the task at hand.

CLASSIC FRENCH FRISÉE SALAD

1 head frisée lettuce (or a combination of escarole and arugula)
¼ lb. (or more!) roquefort cheese, crumbled
½ cup walnuts, toasted and broken into halves
a perfect vinaigrette dressing

Clean the lettuce, break it up, and put it on each of 6 or 8 plates. Distribute the cheese and the walnuts, sprinkle on the dressing, and serve. Serves 6-8.

DON'S INSTANT VINAIGRETTE DRESSING

½ cup wine vinegar, or half balsamic and half lemon juice
4 T. Dijon mustard
½ tsp. salt
freshly ground pepper to taste
4 large cloves garlic
1 cup olive oil

Whip all but the oil in a blender, then slowly add the oil in a thin stream to emulsify. Store the dressing in a jar in the refrigerator. Makes 1½ cups.

Wonderful variation: Use whole pecans instead of walnuts; sauté them in 1 tsp. butter for a minute; then, while they're still in the pan, sprinkle on 2 tsp. sugar, and cook, stirring like mad for another minute, maybe two, until they're caramelized. Put them at once onto a plate to cool, and then use them as your garnish.

YUPPIE PASTA SALAD

1 lb. fresh asparagus, cut into 2" diagonal pieces

1 12-oz. box fusilli or rotini (spiral pasta)

1 smoked chicken breast, or cajun-rubbed, cut into ½" cubes

½ cup sun-dried tomatoes, chopped

vinaigrette dressing (see Classic French Frisée Salad)

1 small log (4-oz.) goat cheese

optional: ¼ cup toasted pine nuts for garnish

Boil the pasta as usual according to the instructions, and pop the asparagus in for the last 5 minutes. Drain, run under cold water to cool, and drain again. In a large bowl, combine the pasta and the asparagus with the smoked chicken and sun-dried tomatoes. Pour the vinaigrette over it, crumble the cheese on top, toss, taste for seasoning, and enjoy with a glass of chilled Pellegrino. Serves 4.

Some of the best and most earth-bound therapy for the elderly is to have a dog or cat to care for. It helps them connect with reality; and the emotional bonds forged with a creature who loves and depends upon them every day for sustenance, make life worth living.

JUDGE'S CHOICE BANGKOK SALAD

12-16 oz. thin egg noodles or Chinese cellophane noodles

½ cup hot broth (chicken or vegetable) or tea

2 T. brown sugar or honey

½ cup peanut butter, creamy or chunky

4 cloves garlic, minced

1 T. fresh ginger, minced

2 T. balsamic vinegar

3 T. soy sauce

1 T. sesame oil

½ tsp. hot sauce or pepper flakes, or to taste

1½ lb. skinless, boneless chicken breasts, poached, cooled, and shredded or cubed, about 4 cups

2 cucumbers, peeled, seeded, grated, & drained in a sieve

1 cup grated fresh peeled carrot

½ cup chopped cilantro for garnish

Cook the noodles according to the package directions; drain, rinse under cold water, and place in a large serving bowl. Meanwhile, make the dressing: dissolve the sugar or honey in the broth or tea and combine it with the next 7 ingredients. Toss the noodles with just enough dressing to moisten well, and reserve. Prepare the rest of the ingredients and serve the salad either in individual soup plates, or in one large bowl or platter – noodles as a base, followed by cucumber, chicken, dressing, carrot, and cilantro. Pass extra dressing on the side. (Vegetarians: omit the chicken.) Serves 6.

Depending on your time and food supplies, the fastest and most delicate Chinese noodles are cellophane or rice noodles. All they need is boiling water poured over them, after which they are left for 10 minutes, drained and used. A great way to serve these noodles is to moisten them with just enough soy sauce to tint them golden bronze. Thin egg noodles, like vermicelli or linguini, are just as good, and they take only a few minutes to cook.

GIRL SCOUT COLESLAW

1 small head of cabbage, shredded

2 carrots, shredded

½ green pepper, seeded and shredded

1 small onion, shredded

¼ cup cider vinegar

3 T. sugar

½-¾ cup mayonnaise

salt to taste

If you have a processer, coleslaw is a snap – 10 minutes, tops. Simply put the vegetables through the machine's shredder, and Bob's your uncle. In a large bowl, sprinkle your shreddings with the vinegar, then the sugar, and toss to combine. This can be done hours or moments before you are ready to serve the slaw; all you need to do then is mix in enough mayonnaise to coat the strands, add salt to taste, and serve. Serves 4-6.

When a young Girl Scout at a camp-out once declined to eat the cole slaw, the leader assured her that this recipe would change her mind. It did, and that coleslaw is now one of that old Girl Scout's most requested pot luck dishes.

A dog likes to obey. It gives them security. James Herriot

ELLEN'S CORN AND BLUE CHEESE SALAD

1 10-oz. package frozen corn, thawed

3 small stalks celery, chopped

1 bunch radishes, trimmed and chopped

1/3 cup red onion, diced

optional: ½ cup fennel, diced

optional: 1 2-oz tin anchovies, drained and chopped

4 T. crumbled blue cheese

1 small head Bibb or Boston lettuce

An hour before you'll need the salad, combine all but the blue cheese and the lettuce with the Ellen's Dressing and set aside. Just before serving, fold in the blue cheese. Serve the salad on a bed of lettuce, or on individual plates on single lettuce leaves. Serves 4-6.

ELLEN'S DRESSING

2 T. wine vinegar

2 T. olive oil

1 T. minced capers

1 T. Dijon mustard

fresh ground pepper to taste

Combine all the ingredients in a jar and serve or refrigerate.

Make radish "mushrooms" by cutting their shapes from fresh radishes — red tops, white stems.

GREEK STYLE POTATO SALAD

3 lb. small new red potatoes, unpeeled, boiled, and halved

2 cloves garlic, peeled

1 T. chopped fresh oregano or marjoram

2 T. red wine vinegar

½ cup olive oil

1 cup (½ lb.) feta cheese, crumbled

salt and pepper to taste

1½ cups Greek olives, pitted

½ cup parsley, finely chopped for garnish

While the potatoes are boiling, char the garlic on a dry skillet very slowly, turning it so that all sides cook evenly. When it is tender and slightly blackened, put it, with the herbs, vinegar, and olive oil into a blender or processer and puree. Add the feta and salt and pepper and blend well. When the potatoes are ready, put them in a serving bowl with the olives, pour on the dressing, and toss. Taste for seasoning, scatter with the parsley, and serve. Serves 6.

A zipped-up duffle bag serves as a handy emergency cat carrier, with the head sticking out, snugged by the zipper.

RED POTATO SALAD WITH RED CAVIAR

2 lb. tiny new red potatoes, washed

1 qt. broth – anything flavorful

2 T. red (whitefish, lumpfish, or salmon) caviar

1/3 cup mayonnaise

½ cup sour cream or yogurt

juice and grated rind of 1 lemon

salt to taste

optional: 4 T. chives, minced, for garnish

Simmer the potatoes in the broth until they're tender – about 10 minutes, while you mix the remaining ingredients for the dressing. Drain the potatoes, cool them for a few minutes, cut them in half, and combine them with their dressing in a serving bowl. Serve them at room temperature, or chill them for later use. (If you're lucky enough to have salmon roe, handle it tenderly when mixing the dressing, and equally carefully when combining the salad and the dressing.) Serves 4.

Every dog should have a man of his own. There is nothing like a well-behaved person around the house to spread the dog's blanket for him or bring him his supper when he comes home man-tired at night. Corey Ford

BREAD SALAD (PANZANELLA)

1 loaf stale Italian or French bread, cut in ½ lengthwise

1 cup broth

1 red or Vidalia onion, sliced thin

5 large perfect, ripe tomatoes in season, diced

4 cloves garlic, minced

½ cup chopped parsley

1 T. fresh basil or rosemary, chopped fine

6 T. olive oil

2 T. wine vinegar

salt and pepper to taste

Sprinkle the broth over the cut sides of the bread. After 10 minutes, squeeze out the excess liquid, discarding it, and cut the bread into small chunks. Meanwhile, put all the other ingredients into a large bowl and mix them well. Add the bread, toss, and taste for seasoning. Serves 8.

A friend of ours, who cannot bear it when the Vidalia onion season comes to an end, has devised a wonderful scheme for extending it; she puts the onions into an old pair of her pantyhose, with a twist-tie between each one. This system keeps them from touching each other in the refrigerator, and they last for months. Really.

A SIMPLE SALAD OF ASPARAGUS
AND BUCKWHEAT NOODLES

1 cup soy sauce

¼ cup strong chicken broth

1 T. sugar

4 T. toasted sesame seeds

1 lb. soba (buckwheat) noodles

1 lb. fresh asparagus, cut on the diagonal into 1" pieces

6 scallions, cut on the diagonal into ½" pieces

fresh mint or basil leaves for garnish

Prepare the dressing by putting in a blender or processer the first 3 ingredients plus 3 tsp. of the sesame seeds (or blend with a whisk). Cook the noodles until they are just tender, adding the asparagus for the last 2 minutes of the boil. Drain them, rinse them with cold water to stop the cooking, and put them into a bowl. Toss them with the dressing and the rest of the sesame seeds, and serve. (If you are an asparagus fan, and the shelves are empty of soba noodles, use vermicelli.) Serves 8-10.

To toast sesame seeds, put them into a small, heavy frying pan over medium heat and stir or shake until they turn golden. Pour them at once onto a cold plate to stop the cooking action.

TAKE-OUT TARRAGON CHICKEN SALAD

1½ stalks celery, coarsely chopped

½ medium onion, coarsely chopped

1 carrot, coarsely chopped

4 T. fresh tarragon, chopped

5 whole peppercorns

1 cup broth, enough to just cover vegetables

2 lb. boneless skinned chicken breasts, poached and cooled

1 cup mayonnaise, more or less, to taste

salt and pepper to taste

Combine the first 6 ingredients in a small saucepan and simmer them, covered, for 15 minutes. Drain and cool the vegetables and puree them in a blender. Chill the puree until you are ready to use it. When you are, cut the chicken breasts into bite-sized pieces. Combine as much of the tarragon puree as you wish with the amount of mayonnaise you need, dress the chicken with it, taste for seasoning, and serve. Serves 6.

Make the vegetable stuff when tarragon is in season, and freeze the puree; it lasts forever.

To please himself only, a cat purrs. Irish Proverb

1 cup fine grade bulghour (cracked wheat)

¼ cup water

6 T. olive oil

4 T. lemon juice

2 tsp. salt

1½ tsp. allspice

2 medium-sized tomatoes, peeled (optional) and finely chopped

1½ cups scallions, finely chopped

1 cup parsley, finely chopped

1 cup mint leaves, finely chopped

romaine leaves or pita bread for serving

Wash the bulghour two or three times in cold water by rinsing it in a fine sieve; drain. In a large bowl, pour the ¼ cup of water over it and let it stand for 1 hour, or until it's light and fluffy, and the water has been absorbed. Mix the dressing and set it aside while you prepare the vegetables; combine everything and serve. Serves 4-6.

The best way to get a puppy is to beg for a baby brother — and they'll settle for a puppy every time. Winston Pendelton

A PILE OF SALAD

2 cups peeled raw beets (¾ lb.), finely shredded

2 cups fresh radishes, finely shredded

2 cups fresh carrots, peeled and finely shredded

2 cups fresh cucumber or cabbage, peeled and finely shredded

1 cup vinaigrette (or your favorite) dressing

parsley, chives, dill, or other fresh herbs for garnish

Using a processer, shred each vegetable separately, and put them in individual bowls so that each can be tossed with ¼ of the dressing. Add whatever extra herb or flavoring you wish to each bowl, e.g., grated ginger to the beets or carrots, dill to the cucumber. Arrange them on a large round serving platter in four wedge shapes, forming a piled circle of separate colors. Use the herb garnish to mark the separations, and to crown the pile. Pea blossoms would be nice. Serves 6-8.

This salad looks just as handsome arranged in stripes on a square or rectangular platter. And using any combo of veggies you like. Vary the dressing, too – a different one for each vegetable?

Those hard-boiled-egg slicers in your kitchen drawer can also be used for slicing mushrooms and kiwi fruit.

CELEBRATION SALAD COMPOSÉE

1 bunch watercress, cleaned, stems removed, rough chopped

1 avocado, peeled and sliced

2 T. smoked mozzarella, shredded

optional: ½ cup thinly sliced red onion

vinaigrette dressing (e.g., Classic French Frisée Salad)

optional: pink peppercorns for garnish

Use the watercress as the base, for four plates of salad, upon which you place the avocado, the onion if you wish, the mozzarella, and your favorite vinaigrette. Garnish it with pink peppercorns, if you can find them, and serve. (If the avocado never got ripe enough, use marinated artichoke hearts.) Serves 4.

Introduce a new pet to an old one gradually. Keep the old pet in one room so that the new one can get used to its smell. Then introduce them through a screen door or a child's gate.

THE MAYO CLINIC: YOU'LL NEVER BUY IT AGAIN

1 egg or egg yolk or eggbeater equivalent

1 T. good olive oil

1 T. Dijon mustard

1 T. lemon juice or vinegar

½ tsp. salt

¼ cup good olive oil

1 cup canola oil, more or less

optional: ½-1 clove garlic, minced, and/or any herb

Into a blender or processer put the first five ingredients and whir for one minute. Then, in a very slow stream, add the quarter cup of olive oil and, when it has been incorporated, add the canola oil, not as slowly. If it seems too thick, add more lemon juice or water. The whole operation will take you about three minutes – five tops, if you include gathering all the ingredients. The great thing about making your own mayonnaise, besides its exquisite taste and the astonishment of your friends, is that you have complete control over its contents. You can use the healthiest oils. You can use eggbeaters if you are leery of using fresh eggs. You can make it chic with sun-dried tomatoes or garlic confit. Canned pimentos turn it a lovely peach color. For a version of aioli, add 6-8 cloves of garlic and 12 drops of hot pepper sauce. When you serve chicken salad, add lots of tarragon and use tarragon vinegar and a little lemon rind; when tomato sandwiches are in season, throw in a handful of fresh basil; creativity is the order of the day. (Once we ran out of canola oil and had to use all olive oil: try that for a heady experience! It was like being in Spain. . .) Makes 1½ cups.

But if you still have a jar of store-bought mayo left in the cupboard, do what Vera does, and add stuff. Into a cup of mayo, she whisks 2 T. lemon juice, 2 T. sour cream, 2 T. eggbeaters, 1 T. Dijon mustard, and 1 small clove of garlic, minced. Uses it for a potato salad with Greek olives, toasted pine nuts and capers.

AFTER BOCCACCIO'S DRESSING

4 oz. blue cheese, crumbled

1½ oz. anchovies (about 10), chopped

½ green pepper, seeded and chopped

½ celery stalk, chopped

¼ onion, chopped

3 sprigs parsley

2 cups olive oil

6 T. white wine vinegar

5 T. Dijon mustard

3 T. red wine vinegar

1 tsp. chopped fresh or ½ tsp. dried basil

½ tsp. coarse ground black pepper

Combine the first 6 ingredients and half the olive oil in a blender. Add the rest and puree. It will keep for weeks in a jar in the refrigerator. Makes 3 cups.

Sir, a woman preaching is like a dog walking on his hind legs. It is not done well; but you are surprised to find it done at all.
Dr. Samuel Johnson

AUGUSTUS CAESAR DRESSING

6 anchovy fillets

1 egg

2 large cloves garlic

¼ cup red wine vinegar

¼ cup lemon juice

¼ cup Parmesan cheese, freshly ground

1 tsp. coarse ground pepper

¼ tsp. salt

2 cups (approximately) olive oil

In a blender or processer, puree the first 3 ingredients. Then add the remaining ingredients except for the olive oil, and combine. With the machine running, pour the oil in a thin stream until the dressing is at about the consistency of heavy cream. Taste for seasoning, and store it, covered, in the refrigerator. Makes 3 cups.

In the winter, rub petroleum jelly on your dog's paws when it goes out in the snow to prevent ice balls from forming between his pads, and to protect his feet from salt on streets.

CILANTRO-LIME SALAD DRESSING

1 large bunch fresh cilantro, stems removed (1/2 cup)

2 cloves garlic, minced

3/4 cup olive oil

zest and juice of 2 limes (2 T.)

salt and pepper to taste

Puree everything in a blender; taste for seasoning and adjust if necessary. Serve it on mixed greens, and top it with a pile of shredded cooked chicken for a nice lunch. (If you want to Tex-Mex it, add ½ cup toasted pumpkin seeds, ½ tsp. hot pepper flakes, and ¼ cup of cream.) It lasts indefinitely in the refrigerator. Makes 2/3 cup.

GOAT CHEESE DRESSING

4 oz. goat cheese (dryish, rather than creamy), crumbled

1/2 cup oil

1/3 cup red wine vinegar

4 T. Dijon mustard

1 clove garlic, minced

salt and pepper to taste

Place all the ingredients in a blender or processer and blend until smooth, or mash them together in a bowl. Chill the dressing until you're ready to use it. Makes 1¼ cups.

Teach a child to leave a dog alone when it's eating or sleeping and never to take away its food.

LOW-FAT GREEN GODDESS DRESSING

1 cup plain low-fat yogurt

1 tsp. fresh tarragon, chopped

2 T. tarragon or wine vinegar

1 scallion, minced

1½ T. parsley, minced

2 tsp. anchovy paste or finely chopped anchovy fillets

2 tsp. sugar

½ tsp. salt

Combine all the ingredients in a bowl, blender, or processer, blending well. Chill the dressing, covered, for at least 2 hours before serving. Makes 1½ cups.

GINGER YOGURT DRESSING

1¼ cups plain yogurt

¼ cup crystallized ginger, chopped

1 T. honey

Combine all the ingredients in a jar and serve or refrigerate. Very nice on fresh fruit. Makes about 1 ½ cups.

The cat is a dilettante in fur. Théophile Gautier

VEGETABLES

10 Reasons Besides Popcorn to Own
a Microwave Oven

1   Meat loaf or coq au vin in 20 minutes

2   Softens hard brown sugar and decrystallizes honey

3   The best vegetables you ever tasted in no time at all: dreamy broccoli in 2 minutes; peel 'n' eat corn on the cob in 2 minutes; artichokes in 9 minutes; baked potatoes, 3 to 5 each; and peeled tomatoes or peaches in 15 seconds

4   Warming plates for a dinner party: sprinkle with water, stack, and heat for about 3 minutes

5   Perfect poached fish every time

6   Brings cold cheese to room temp in 15 seconds

7   Glorious chicken broth from scratch and scraps in minutes (save those bones!)

8   Keeps the kitchen cool in summer and saves energy all year

9   For toasting nuts, crisping potato chips and crackers, etc.

10 To hasten the rising of bread: read the directions that come with your oven.

11 (We had to add this one: to remove a stamp from an envelope, put 3 drops of water on it, and microwave for 30 seconds.)

DOUBLE-COOKED MAINE POTATOES FOR SUNDAY

2 T. olive oil

2 large onions, thinly sliced

1/4 cup white wine

4 large Maine potatoes, peeled and sliced into 1/4" slices

2 cups broth

salt and pepper to taste

1/3 cup bread crumbs, preferably freshly made

Heat the oil in a cast-iron skillet, add the onions, and sauté for about 5 minutes, stirring, until soft and golden. Toss in the wine, stir it for a minute and add the potatoes. Pour in the broth, season with salt and pepper, stir to mix, and turn down the heat. Cook for about 15 minutes, or until the potatoes are tender and the broth has been absorbed, stirring once or twice. Towards the end of the simmering, preheat the broiler, and when the potatoes are ready, sprinkle them with the crumbs and pop them under the broiler for a minute, until they are crusty and browned. Serves 4-6.

ROASTED RESTAURANT POTATOES

8 unpeeled (optional) potatoes

8-10 cloves garlic

butter for the baking pan

4 T. olive oil

salt and pepper to taste

In a large pot, combine the potatoes and garlic with water to cover, and simmer for 20 minutes, until tender. Drain them; chop and reserve the garlic. Preheat the oven to 425 and generously butter a shallow baking dish. When the potatoes are cool enough to handle (don't let them get cold), chop them roughly, pack them into the baking dish, sprinkle the garlic, olive oil, and salt and pepper over the top, and roast them for about 20 minutes, or until they look brown and crisp. Serves 8.

GARLIC SMASHED POTATOES: AN ALL-TIME FAVE

    potatoes, as many as you wish

    garlic, 1-3 peeled cloves for every spud (don't be shy – you won't
        be sorry!)

    milk, broth, or water to cover

    olive oil

    salt and pepper to taste

    optional: sour cream, and about 1/3 cup grated Parmesan

Prepare the potatoes for boiling, peeling if you wish, and put them in a saucepan with the garlic, barely covering them with the liquid you have chosen. Boil them until tender and drain them, saving the liquid. With an electric beater, begin to mash them, slowly adding a little olive oil, a little of the cooking liquid, a little more olive oil, etc., until you like the consistency. Season to taste and serve at once. Serves any number.

If you want to gild the lily, add the sour cream instead of your reserved liquid with the oil, season the mixture, and top it with the grated Parmesan. Pop it under a low broiler for a few minutes, watching it carefully. It should puff up; serve it at once.

A man can do worse sometimes than follow a tip his dog gives him.
Albert Payson Terhune

CORINNE'S EASTER POTATOES

2¼ lb. new potatoes, washed and dried

4 T. olive oil

4 large cloves garlic, chopped roughly

1 - 3 branches fresh rosemary, snipped into ½" pieces

salt and pepper to taste

1/3 cup dry white wine

9 oz. green and black olives, pitted and chopped roughly

If the potatoes are large, cut them into wedges. Heat the oil in a large non-stick frying pan and sauté the garlic and rosemary for one minute. Add the potatoes and the salt and pepper and sauté, stirring until the potatoes are golden and glazed. Add the wine, cover the pan, and cook for 15 minutes on low heat, stirring occasionally. Put the olives into boiling water for 10 seconds and then cool them under cold water. Add them to the potatoes, cook five minutes more, and serve. Serves 6-8.

A dog starv'd at his master's gate predicts the ruin of the state.
William Blake

INCENDIARY POTATO SHARDS

4 large baking potatoes, scrubbed, unpeeled

¼ cup oil

8 large cloves garlic, minced

4 T. fresh lime juice

2 tsp. Tabasco

½ tsp. hot pepper flakes

salt to taste

Cut each potato into 8 long wedges. In a small bowl, blend all the other ingredients. Taste for salt. Put the potatoes in a large baking dish, and pour on all but ¼ of the dressing, tossing to coat. Let them stand for 30 minutes. Meanwhile, preheat the oven to 400. Bake the potatoes for 40 minutes, turning once in a while, until golden and soft. Sprinkle the remaining dressing over them and serve. Serves 6-8.

If you find a cat or dog that can't get up after an accident, very carefully slip it onto a board or a blanket or coat held taut for a stretcher, and get it to a vet immediately.

3 large sweet potatoes, washed and cut into 1/2" slices

2 T. oil

coarse salt and cracked pepper to taste

Toss the potato slices in a bowl with the oil until just covered and grill or broil them for about 10 minutes, turning several times, until they are tender. Serve immediately. (A variation of these is to roast them in the oven, and to cut the slices into 1/2" sticks, tossing them in the same mixture but adding ¾ tsp. hot pepper flakes. Preheat the oven to 400, and roast them for 30-40 minutes, turning them once in the process.) Serves 4.

Save some of your 500 milligram vitamin-C pills to crush and mix with olive oil and fresh herbs in a blender — one pill for every 6 ounces of oil. The color will stay green forever if you keep it in the refrigerator, and you will have fabulous oil for salads, pastas, pizzas, etc. The discovery of brilliant chef David Bouley.

ROASTED CARROTS

1-2 lb. carrots, shredded

4 T. butter

salt and pepper to taste

Place an 8-inch cast-iron frying pan on the stove, fill it with the carrots, and cook them on high heat, turning with a spatula so that they will begin to dehydrate and darken evenly. When some of them begin to turn black and the rest seem well dried out and cooked, reduce the heat, add the butter, salt, and pepper, and stir to blend. Serve the carrots in a warm dish. Serves 4-6.

VODKA CARROTS: 15 CALORIES PER PERSON!

1 lb. carrots, peeled and sliced thinly on the diagonal

1 orange: zest and juice

1/3 cup vodka

¼ tsp. nutmeg

pinch of salt and sugar

Combine all of the ingredients in a saucepan, add water if necessary, and cook for about 7 minutes, until the carrots are crisp-tender. Serves 4.

CRACKED PEPPER CARROTS

1 lb. baby carrots

1 T. butter

1 T. brown sugar or honey

¼ tsp. cracked black pepper

Combine all of the ingredients in a saucepan with ½ cup of water, cover, bring to a boil, and simmer for 5 minutes or until tender. Season and serve. Serves 4.

ZUCCHINI GUADALAJARA

1 small onion, chopped

2 - 3 T. oil

2 cups zucchini, skin on, cut into 1" cubes

2 cups white corn kernels, fresh, canned, or frozen and thawed

1 poblano chili, roasted and diced, seeded, and peeled

   or

½ green bell pepper and 2 jalapeños, seeded and chopped

salt and pepper to taste

1 cup pepper jack cheese, shredded

In a large skillet, sauté the onion in a bit of the oil, and then add the zucchini for a few minutes and finally the corn for 1 minute – a total of 5-6 minutes. Season with the pepper and salt, scatter the cheese on top, cover the pan, and cook long enough for the cheese to melt while the vegetables steam – 4-5 minutes more. Serves 4.

(To roast the poblano, heat it on all sides on a flat tin surface, until it's suitably blackened. Pop it into a paper bag for a minute to steam, and when you remove it, the skin will come off easily.)

What in hell have I done to deserve all these kittens? Don Marquis

ZUCCHINI WITH PESTO MCGUIRE

2 lb. zucchini, peel on, cut into sticks

2 - 4 T. olive oil

2 - 4 T. pesto sauce

salt and pepper to taste

optional: pine nuts, toasted, for garnish

Sauté the zucchini in the olive oil in a large skillet for 1-2 minutes – until it's just tender. Stir in 2 T. pesto and toss well, adding more pesto or olive oil if necessary. Season with salt and pepper, and garnish with the pine nuts. Serves 4.

NEVER-FAIL ZUCCHINI SOUFFLÉ

1 lb. zucchini, peeled, cubed, and cooked until tender

1   3-oz. package cream cheese

1 T. feta cheese, crumbled

1 egg, lightly beaten

optional: 2 T. onion or shallot, finely chopped

salt and pepper to taste

buttered bread crumbs

Preheat the oven to 350. Mash the zucchini with a fork while it's still warm, add the cheeses and blend. Add the egg (and optional onion or shallots) and the salt and pepper. Pour the soufflé into a 2-quart buttered casserole, sprinkle the bread crumbs on top, and bake it for 30-40 minutes, until it's golden and bubbly. Serves 4.

Go anywhere in England where there are natural, wholesome, contented, and really nice English people; and what do you always find? That the stables are the real center of the household.
George Bernard Shaw

ZUCCHINI CRUST PIZZA

3 cups grated zucchini, drained and squeezed dry

3 eggs, well beaten

½ cup flour

¼ tsp. salt

1 medium tomato, thinly sliced

6-8 oz. mozzarella cheese, shredded

½ cup Greek olives, chopped

2/3 cup scallions, minced

8 - 10 fresh basil leaves, or 2 tsp. dried basil

salt, slivered garlic, and olive oil for sprinkling on top

Preheat oven to 450. Combine zucchini pulp with eggs, flour, and salt. Oil a pizza pan, spread zucchini mix in an even layer, and bake for 8 minutes. Remove from oven and turn the temperature down to 350. Lay the tomatoes over the top, and add the rest of the ingredients. (If you want to cut down on cheese, use half, and add it 5 minutes before the end.) Bake the pizza for 20 minutes, or until the cheese is melted and the base is set. Serves 4-6.

If there are lots of fresh, dry, clean basil leaves left, save them for future use by packing them in a jar and covering them with olive oil. They'll stay fresh-flavored for many months in the refrigerator, and you can use the scented oil for salads, bread dipping, pizza sprinkling – all sorts of things.

Before travelling with a pet overnight, freeze water in a plastic bowl with a cover, and keep several refills in the freezer.

IOLE'S STUFFED TOMATOES

4 fresh summer tomatoes

4 T. raw rice

2 cloves garlic, minced

2 T. fresh basil, chopped

2 T. olive oil

pinch of sugar

salt and pepper to taste

extra olive oil for sprinkling

Preheat the oven to 350. Cut a slice off the bottom (not the stem end) of each tomato, and save it. Scoop out the seeds and juice and reserve the juice. In a small bowl, combine the rest of the ingredients plus ¼ cup of the reserved juice, and divide it among the four tomatoes. Add a few drops of oil to each, top with its lid, and place in an oiled baking dish. Cover them with foil, bake for one hour, and serve lukewarm. Serves 4.

These delicious tomatoes are served by an Italian professor every year during tomato season. If you have any sort of pesto on hand, red, green, or brown, try using it instead – about 2 T. per recipe – with the rice and the juice. It's a time saver, and a wonderful variation.

Nobody ever sold eleven puppies before noon on Sunday.
Eileen Schroeder

STUFFED TOMATOES ACAPULCO

6 ripe tomatoes

3 cups corn, fresh or frozen (thawed)

1 green pepper, seeded and chopped

1 jalapeño pepper, seeded and minced

3 T. scallions, chopped

1 T. fresh basil, chopped

2 T. fresh cilantro, chopped

¼ lb. pepper jack cheese, grated coarsely

salt and pepper to taste

4 T. breadcrumbs (any kind, but stale corn bread would be nice)

1 T. butter

cooking spray

Preheat the oven to 400. Cut a slice off the smooth bottom of each tomato and save the slices for lids. Scoop out the insides and reserve half of them in a bowl, and turn the tomatoes over to drain. Add to the pulp in the bowl everything but the crumbs and butter. Toss the stuffing gently, and fill the tomato cavities loosely. Scatter the crumbs on top, and dot each one with butter. Spray a baking sheet and place the tomatoes on it with their lids beside them, skin up. Bake for 20-25 minutes, until the tomatoes are cooked and the tops crisp. Serve at once, or cool them and take them on a picnic. Serves 6.

In a new home, a cat will often vanish. It is actually hiding in a dark corner until it feels safe. When the house is quiet and less threatening, the cat will reappear.

ROAST TOMATOES WITH TOMATO CRUMBS FOR A CROWD

8 cloves garlic, unpeeled

olive oil for sprinkling

½ cup Italian parsley, finely chopped

1 cup fresh unseasoned bread crumbs (make in the processer)

¼ cup olive oil

30 fresh plum tomatoes, cut in half lengthwise

10 sun-dried tomatoes, not in oil, ground in a blender

salt and pepper to taste

Preheat the oven to 375. Put the garlic in a pie plate, sprinkle the cloves with the olive oil, and bake for 10 minutes or until soft. Cool, peel, and mash with a fork. Put the paste in a small bowl with the parsley, bread crumbs, and the ¼ cup of olive oil, and mix them together. Place the tomatoes, skin side down, in a roasting pan and sprinkle them with the breadcrumbs and then the sun-dried tomato crumbs. Roast them for 15 or 20 minutes, or until they are soft but not falling apart, and serve at once. Serves 10-15.

To make your own dried plum tomatoes, trim their stem ends, lightly massage them with oil, halve them lengthwise, and place them, skin side down, on wire racks on cookie sheets. Sprinkle them with salt, pepper and minced herbs and/or garlic on the middle rack of a 200 degree oven for 6-8 hours, until they are half their original size and still soft. You can do this while you sleep, and you can also treat apricots, peaches, plums, mangos, papayas and pineapple this way. Refrigerated in a covered container, they will last for up to a week; covered with oil, longer. If you dry them in a 150 degree oven for 12-24 hours, layer them with fresh basil, and cover them with oil in a jar in the refrigerator, they'll last for months.

The smallest feline is a masterpiece. Leonardo da Vinci

VIDALIA ONION TART

½ cup sugar

1 T. butter

6 Vidalia or other sweet onions, halved, then sliced thinly

pinch of salt

single pastry crust

Preheat the oven to 425. Spray a non-stick tart pan or skillet with vegetable oil, put the sugar and butter in it and heat it slowly for 5-10 minutes, until they're caramelized. Arrange the onions on top of the caramel layer, sprinkle with salt, and cover with the pie crust. Bake the tart for 25 minutes, until the crust is done, and then place the pan on a burner over high heat for 2 minutes to brown the bottom, turning it around often, and loosening the contents with a spatula before you invert it onto a plate, and serve it. Serves 6-8

The best way to cover a hole in the upholstery is to cover it with a snoozing schnauzer.

ARTICHOKE BOTTOMS AND BEANS À LA GRECQUE

juice of 2 lemons

2 T. flour

6 fresh artichoke bottoms, chokes removed

2 - 3 T. olive oil

2 cloves garlic, crushed

1 onion, chopped

1 lb. lima beans, fresh, or frozen and thawed

1 tsp. sugar

salt and pepper to taste

chopped fresh dill or parsley and lemon wedges for garnish

In a deep bowl, combine the juice of 1 lemon and the flour with a whisk, and slowly add a quart of water and a pinch of salt. As you prepare the artichoke bottoms, rub them with a lemon half, cut them in large pieces, and drop them into the bowl. Put them on to simmer, covered, in a pan with 1 cup of their liquid and the rest of the lemon juice. Meanwhile, in a large frying pan, heat the oil, and sauté the garlic and the onion until they are golden. Pour in 2 cups of the flour water, whisk until smooth, and add the beans and sugar, simmering until soft, about 5 minutes. Roughly chop the artichoke bottoms, add them with their liquid to this mixture, and continue cooking until they are soft. Serve them garnished with the chopped herbs and lemon wedges. Serves 4.

Honest as the cat when the meat is out of reach. English Proverb

PASTA
·&·
GRAINS

10 While-the-Pasta-is-Cooking Toppings

1   Scrub and de-beard 2 lb. of cultured mussels, and steam them in a pot with a small can of marinara sauce until they open. Serve, shells and all, European style, garnished with parsley.

2   Sauté a few slivered cloves of garlic for 30 seconds in olive oil, swirl in ½ cup red wine, then add half of a 28-oz. can of crushed tomatoes. Simmer it while you puree a cup of pitted Greek olives to dollop on top of the sauce.

3   Sauté some tiny scallops for 1 minute in butter, roll them in ground toasted walnuts, and use them as a topping sprinkled with chopped parsley. (Return the drained pasta to its pot with a little cream and broth, swirling the contents together for a few minutes to thicken the dish; then serve it with the scallops on top.)

4   Sauté 3 or 4 minced garlic cloves in olive oil and add 2 cans of shrimp (4¼-oz.) or ½ lb. of fresh, peeled, heating them briefly. Add 2 T. vodka or dry white wine. Garnish with chopped parsley.

5   In a large skillet, quickly brown 6 slivered cloves of garlic with the entire contents of a can of anchovy fillets, or with ¾ cup of pine nuts and some olive oil. Swirl in the zest and juice of a lemon. The cooked pasta is added to the skillet with a bit of its broth, tossed to mix, and garnished with toasted bread crumbs.

6   Boil a few Italian sausages with the pasta, and meanwhile, sauté a couple of chopped onions. Skin and chop the sausage, add it to the onions with a can of chopped tomatoes and cook to blend.

7   Mix chopped artichoke hearts, sun-dried tomatoes, and pitted Greek olives, and garnish with grated lemon rind and fresh basil.

8   Combine ¼ lb. blue cheese with ¼ cup cream and 2 T. dry wine or vermouth. Drain the pasta, put it into a large pan, and reheat it with the cheese mixture plus lots of black pepper.

9   Use any kind of pesto mixed with some of the spaghetti liquid, plus cooked leftover meat, chicken, or chorizo, sliced. Top it with chopped fresh herbs to match and grated cheese.

10   Do it Chinese style, with either fresh asparagus spears, broccoli florets, or peas sautéed quickly in a bit of sesame oil with toasted sesame seeds and hot pepper flakes. When you toss in the drained pasta, add broth or cream and blend.

SHELLS WITH LOBSTER AND HOT PEPPERS

12 oz. medium size shells

4 T. olive oil

4 red or green jalapeño peppers, seeded and diced fine

1 red bell pepper, diced

4 garlic cloves, chopped

2 medium tomatoes, diced

peel of 1 lemon, grated coarsely

2 cups cooked lobster, cut into bite size pieces

¼ cup fresh parsley, chopped

olive oil and lemon wedges for garnish

Cook the pasta as indicated on the package, and keep it warm. Meanwhile, heat the oil in a large skillet and sauté the peppers and garlic for about 3 minutes, until they're soft. Add the tomatoes and the lemon peel and cook for another 10 minutes; then put in the lobster for the last minute or two, to heat it through. Combine everything with the pasta and parsley, taste for seasoning, and serve with a splash of olive oil and the lemon wedges. Serves 4.

When blueberries are in season, freeze them on cookie sheets. They can then be stored in the freezer in 1 cup portions in small plastic bags for future use — no need to measure, nor to thaw.

PAUL'S PASTA VONGOLE WITH CILANTRO

3 cups raw pasta: rotini, shells, linguine, etc.

2 T. olive oil

6-8 cloves garlic, chopped

2 huge bunches fresh cilantro, washed and chopped

1 jalapeño pepper, seeded and chopped

2 cans (6½ oz.) chopped or minced clams in clam juice

lots of black pepper, fresh ground

Cook the pasta as the package directs. Meanwhile, in a large skillet, heat the oil and sauté the garlic, cilantro, and jalapeño about 5 minutes, over medium heat, until the garlic is golden. Add the clam juice and simmer until the pasta is ready to drain. When it is drained, turn up the heat under the skillet and add the clams and black pepper, stirring them for about 2 minutes. To serve, put the pasta into warmed plates and top with the clam sauce. Serves 3.

The spin on this nifty sauce is the cilantro, but of course you may use parsley if cilantro is as hard to find as it sometimes is in Maine.

In an emergency, a good strong dog leash can be used as a horse lead, and vice versa.

PASTA SCAMPI ROSSI

2 12-oz. packages spaghetti or linguini

2 lb. medium shrimp, shelled and deveined

½ cup olive oil

½ cup dry vermouth

4 cloves garlic, crushed

¾ tsp. salt

½ tsp. pepper

3 T. parsley for garnish

3 T. lemon juice

Boil the pasta according to the package directions, and while it is cooking, prepare the rest. Quickly sauté the shrimp in the olive oil; when they turn pink, remove them right away and reserve. Add the vermouth, garlic, and salt and pepper to the pan and cook until the liquid is reduced by half. Return the shrimp briefly to the pan to warm them and mix them with the sauce. Drain the pasta and arrange it on a platter; put the shrimp on top and sprinkle with the parsley and lemon juice before serving. Serves 6-8.

When fresh herbs are plentiful, one way of freezing them is to pack the washed leaves into 5-oz. paper cups, fill them with water, and freeze them. When you need them, defrost them under cold water and treat them like fresh herbs.

JOAN'S FAVORITE ALL-SEASON SPAGHETTI

1 lb. pasta: fettuccine or linguine

4 T. olive oil

2 cloves garlic, minced

2 T. fresh (or 2 tsp. dried) basil, chopped

¼ tsp. red pepper flakes

1 pint cherry tomatoes, whole

1 small bunch broccoli, cut into 1" florets

½ cup broth

¼ tsp. salt

¼ cup Parmesan, grated

¼ cup fresh parsley, chopped

½ cup walnuts, toasted and chopped, for garnish

Put the fettuccine on to cook, following the package directions. Meanwhile, in a large frying pan, put 2 T. of the oil and the garlic, basil, and pepper flakes. Add the tomatoes and sauté over low heat for about 5 minutes, stirring often; they will wilt. Remove from the heat, cover, and keep warm. Add the broccoli to the pasta for its last 5 minutes of cooking time and drain them together in a colander. Put the rest of the oil into the spaghetti pot, and return the pasta and broccoli. Add the tomatoes, ¼ cup of the broth, the salt, the Parmesan, and the parsley. Toss, adding more broth if needed, and serve at once, sprinkled with the walnuts. Pass extra cheese at the table, if you like. Serves 4-5.

Whenever nuts are called for in a recipe, try to toast them first – the flavor is twice as intense.

SHELLS WITH VODKA, HOT SAUCE, GOAT CHEESE, AND OPTIONAL SCALLOPS

12 oz. pasta shells

2 T. olive oil

4 large cloves garlic, minced

2 large fresh tomatoes, roughly chopped

optional: ½ lb. fresh scallops

4 oz. goat cheese

¼ cup cream, any kind

¼ cup vodka (pepper vodka, if you have it)

1 tsp. hot pepper sauce, or to taste

salt and pepper to taste

1 T. fresh basil, chopped, for garnish

Put the spaghetti on to cook and drain, following your usual method. Meanwhile, in a large frying pan, heat the olive oil, add the garlic, and sauté a minute until golden. Add the tomatoes and cook a few more minutes. Put in the scallops, and add, a dab at a time, the cheese and the cream, cooking and mixing until blended. The vodka goes in next, and then the hot sauce, while the scallops finish cooking. Taste for seasoning, and pour the sauce over the over the hot spaghetti and garnish with basil. Serves 4.

Instead of the scallops, you might try asparagus or sugar snap peas cut into 1" diagonal pieces, dropped into the spaghetti water for the last 2 minutes, and reserved with the drained pasta.

To his dog, every man is Napoleon; hence the constant popularity of dogs. Aldous Huxley

FRESH CABBAGE FETTUCCINE

1 large onion, chopped

4-5 T. olive oil, butter, or bacon fat

1 small (2-3 lb.) cabbage, cored and shredded

½ tsp. hot pepper flakes, or to taste

2 T. white wine, beer, or broth

12 oz. fettuccine, cooked, drained, and kept warm

salt and pepper to taste

In a large frying pan, sauté the onion in the olive oil. Turn up the heat, add the cabbage and the pepper flakes, and sauté until they are lightly browned, about 7 minutes. Add the liquid, cover, and simmer for about 5 more minutes until the cabbage is tender. When the cabbage is ready, add the fettuccine to the frying pan and blend everything together, tasting for salt and pepper. (For a Hungarian touch, forget the hot pepper flakes – this dish could be garnished with thinned sour cream and paprika. Or, for a different slant, you might use fennel seeds – lightly toasted in a frying pan – instead of the hot pepper flakes.) Serves 4.

Everyone who has ever made this dish has expressed surprise at how quick and easy it is to make, but most of all, how delicious it is, which is rather nice, since cabbage is always in season.

I myself have known some very profoundly thoughtful dogs.
James Thurber

RICHARD'S PREFERRED PASTA: ALLA CARBONARA

2 T. butter
2 T. olive oil
3 slices bacon, diced
½ cup fine strips of ham
2 eggs
2/3 cup cheese, grated (half Parmesan, half Romano)
1 lb. spaghetti
salt and pepper to taste

Heat together in a large frying pan, over moderate heat, the butter and the oil; add the bacon and the ham. Meanwhile, put the spaghetti on to cook; follow package directions. Whisk the eggs and cheese together and reserve. When the bacon has barely begun to brown, remove the pan from the fire and stir in the egg mixture very quickly. Drain and add the hot spaghetti and blend; season with the salt and lots of freshly ground pepper and serve at once. Serves 4-5.

If there is anything leftover, try making a lunch of fried carbonara cakes: heat some oil (or butter – it browns better) in a large frying pan and, taking a handful of the leftover spaghetti, form a 4" patty. Brown it on both sides in the oil and keep it warm in the oven on paper towels until you've used all of the leftover pasta.

Properly trained, a man can be dog's best friend. Corey Ford

PASTA WITH CHICK PEAS

3 cups pasta: penne, ditalini, shells, etc.

1 19-oz. can chick peas, drained and divided in half

2 T. olive oil

2 large cloves garlic, minced

2 sprigs dry rosemary

1 T. tomato paste

2 tsp. anchovy paste, or to taste

1 cup canned tomatoes, crushed or pureed

1 cup broth

Parmesan cheese, shaved, for garnish

Put the pasta on to cook, according to the package directions. Meanwhile, puree half of the chick peas in a blender or processer. Heat the oil in a large frying pan, add the garlic, and sauté gently. When it's tender (about 1 minute), add the rest of the ingredients except for the whole chick peas, and cook together for 10 or 15 minutes, until well blended. When the pasta is done, drain it and add it with the whole chick peas to the pan, warming everything briefly before sprinkling with the Parmesan and serving. This dish could also be garnished with chopped Greek olives or fresh herbs. Serves 4.

Cats seem to go on the principal that it never does any harm to ask for what you want. Joseph Wood Krutch

CORKSCREWS WITH CAULIFLOWER

1 lb. fusilli or rotini (corkscrew pasta)

1 head cauliflower, about 2 lb., cut into florets

1/3 cup olive oil

6 large cloves garlic, minced

6 anchovy fillets, drained

optional: ½ tsp. hot pepper flakes

fresh breadcrumbs browned in olive oil for garnish

Put the pasta on to boil according to the directions and, while it's cooking (in the same water, if you like) briefly blanch the cauliflower and chop it coarsely. Heat the olive oil in a large skillet, add the pepper flakes if desired, and sauté the garlic until it's blonde. Add the anchovies, mashing them as they cook for about a minute, and then add the cauliflower, mixing everything well. Toss it with the pasta in a large bowl, and sprinkle with the breadcrumbs. Serves 6.

If a dog is protecting his property, do not look him directly in the eyes; always avert your eyes from meeting his gaze.

SPAGHETTI WITH ALL SORTS OF 'SHROOMS

2 T. olive oil

1 large red onion, slivered

2 large cloves garlic, minced

1 pound mushrooms, as interesting as you can find (shitake, portobello, oyster, chanterelles, etc.), thinly sliced

1 cup very dry white wine

½ cup broth

1 lb. pasta: penne, fusilli, or fettuccine

1 T. butter

1 T. dried marjoram

2 T. fresh parsley, chopped

1 T. freshly ground black pepper (yes!)

salt to taste

good Parmesan cheese, shaved, for garnish

In a large frying pan, sauté the onions and the garlic until they wilt. Add the mushrooms, in two batches, and sauté until all are incorporated. This will take about 10 minutes. When they begin to absorb their juices, add the white wine and the broth and allow all to simmer for about 45 minutes, until everything has shriveled and the sauce looks nicely cooked. Meanwhile, cook the pasta, drain it, and place it on a large, heated platter. Just before serving, add the butter and flavorings and toss. Serve with Parmesan shavings. Serves 4.

Dried mushrooms, soaked in warm water and carefully cleaned, can be used as part of this dish.

Acquiring a dog may be the only opportunity a human ever has to choose a relative. Mordecai Siegal

W'S FAVE: RAW TOMATO SAUCE FOR PASTA

2 lb. very ripe tomatoes, peeled, seeded, and chopped

2 cloves garlic, minced

¼ cup fresh basil leaves (about 20) cut up with scissors

optional: ½ lb. fresh mozzarella, sliced or shredded

5 T. olive oil

salt and pepper to taste

1 lb. penne or ziti

Combine all except the pasta in a large serving bowl an hour before eating, and let it stand to fuse the flavors. Just before the meal, cook the pasta and, while it's cooking, warm the plates. Drain the pasta, mix it with the sauce, and serve at once. Serves 4.

Have you ever thought of trying a double-crust pizza? Make the usual dough (or buy it in a lump) and use a large oiled cake pan. Spread 2/3 of the dough on the bottom and up its sides, and save the rest, in the shape of a circle the size of the pan, for the top. Fill the pizza with cheese and tons of mushrooms, or cooked sausage, and fit the top over it, sealing the edges with water. Smear the top with tomato sauce, like frosting, and bake the pizza as usual. Turn it out of its pan, slice it in wedges, and serve.

BEANS AND BOWS WITH BROCCOLI RABE

12 oz. farfalle, or bow-tie pasta

6 T. olive oil

2 cloves garlic, minced

1 tsp. red pepper flakes, crushed

1½ lb. broccoli rabe, about 2 bunches, washed and trimmed

1 16-oz. can white beans, drained and rinsed

optional: 1 T. fresh basil or 1 tsp. fresh rosemary, chopped

¼ cup Romano or Pecorino cheese, shaved

Prepare the pasta as directed on the package. While the pasta is cooking, heat the oil in a large skillet and sauté the garlic with the pepper flakes until the garlic is fragrant but not golden. Tear or cut the rabe into small pieces, add it to the skillet, and sauté for 2 minutes, until it's wilted. Add the beans and the optional herbs and simmer for 5 more minutes. When the pasta is al dente, drain it and toss it with the cheese in a warm platter. Pile the beans and broccoli on top and serve. Serves 4-6.

You can capture a cat by throwing a towel over it. If it is injured, wrap the towel around it and carry it by supporting its head and neck with one hand; the rest of its body with the other. Use a towel also when giving a cat pills — to avoid scratches.

LEFTOVER SPAGHETTI FRITTATA WITH LEFTOVERS

3 cups leftover spaghetti, cooked

4 eggs, beaten lightly

1/3 cup Parmesan or Romano cheese, grated

4 oz. anything in the fridge: crabmeat, olives, roasted garlic, mushrooms, anchovies, tuna, or a combination

salt and pepper to taste

2 T. olive oil or butter

Fast version: mix the first 4 ingredients in a bowl and add salt and pepper to taste. Put the olive oil into a 12" non-stick skillet with a heatproof handle, heat it, and add the mixture. Cook over medium heat, moving the pan so that each part of it remains over the center of the heat for 2 minutes, until the bottom is set and the top is still a little soft, about 10 minutes. Meanwhile, turn on the broiler, and when it's ready, put the pan under it and heat until set, about 2 or 3 more minutes. Serves 4.

Baked version: preheat the oven to 375; butter a flat baking dish and coat it with breadcrumbs or Parmesan. Mix the first 4 ingredients in a bowl, season the mixture, and pour it into the baking dish. Drizzle with olive oil, and bake for 25 to 30 minutes, until just set and browned. Serve at once; or cool for a few minutes, turn out of the pan, and serve.

I was one of the luckier women who came to motherhood with some experience. I owned a Yorkshire terrier for three years.
Erma Bombeck

LEMON RISOTTO

5 cups chicken stock

2 shallots, minced

1 T. olive oil

4 T. sweet butter

1½ cups arborio rice

leaves from 2 sprigs thyme, chopped

leaves from 1 sprig rosemary, chopped

leaves from 1 sprig mint or sage, chopped

rind of 1 lemon, grated

3 T. lemon juice

½ cup grated Parmesan

Heat the chicken stock. Meanwhile, in a heavy-bottomed pan, gently sauté the shallots in the olive oil and 2 tablespoons of the butter for 2 or 3 minutes. Add the rice and continue to cook over low heat, stirring from time to time, until the rice is shiny and translucent. Add a ladleful of stock and stir for 1 or 2 minutes, until it's absorbed; then add another. Keep stirring and adding ladlefuls of stock as each amount is gradually absorbed into the rice; this should take about 20 minutes. Remove from the heat and add the remaining butter, the chopped herbs, the lemon juice and rind, and the Parmesan. Wait 2 minutes for the flavors to penetrate, taste for seasoning, and then serve right away. Serves 4-6.

If you're lucky enough to have any left over the next day, form it into a patty and heat a frying pan the proper size to hold it. Put in about a tablespoon of butter, and when it is hot, put the pancake in, press it down as it browns, and turn it with a large spatula to brown and crisp the other side. Have it for lunch.

MICROWAVE RISOTTO

1 tsp. olive oil

1 tsp. sweet butter

4 T. onion or shallot, chopped

½ cup arborio rice

2 T. dry white wine

1½ cups broth, vegetable or meat

1 tsp. sweet butter

2 T. freshly ground Parmesan cheese

coarse salt and freshly ground pepper to taste

This recipe is for a 600-700 watt microwave oven. In a shallow 8" or 9" glass dish, heat the oil and butter together for 1 minute (always on HIGH; always uncovered), or until the butter is melted. Add the onion, stir, and cook for 2 minutes. Add the rice and the wine and cook for 3 minutes, or until the wine evaporates. Add the broth and cook for 16 minutes, stirring once halfway through the cooking. Two minutes before the end of the cooking, stir in the cheese. Let the dish stand uncovered for 3 minutes before serving it, stirring several times to let the rice absorb all of the liquid. Try putting a dollop of any kind of pesto in the center and dragging it towards the edges in 6 or 8 lines, making a giant star – or creating a spiral pattern. Serves 2.

The reason people rave about using the microwave for risotto is not time, but because it saves stirring, and it produces a splendid dish. Vary the liquids, add seafood, vegetables and other flavorings or herbs (fresh ones, 2 minutes before the end of the cooking, dried, 4 minutes before the end). One combination is ¼ lb. fresh asparagus cut into ½" pieces, plus 2 T. shredded smoked mozzarella, added halfway through the last stage, when you stop to stir. To double the recipe, multiply by two, use a larger dish, cook the butter for 2 minutes, the onion for 4 minutes, the wine for 5, and the rest for 24 minutes, stirring once after 12 minutes. We are grateful to Barbara Kafka for introducing her method into our lives. Look up her fabulous versions in her MICROWAVE GOURMET cookbook.

RICARDO'S DIRTY GREEN RICE

1¾ cups broth or water

1 poblano or 3 jalapeño chilis, seeded and chopped fine

1 small bunch fresh cilantro, chopped fine

4 or 5 green scallion tops, chopped fine

1 cup raw rice

salt and pepper to taste

Put the first 4 ingredients into a blender or processer and puree them. In a saucepan, bring the green liquid to a boil (you will need 2 cups, so add water if necessary), add the rice, bring it back to a boil, and turn it down at once to low heat. Cover the pan and let the rice simmer ever so gently for 20 minutes. Taste for seasoning and serve. Serves 4.

To make the green liquid, you can use anything you have on hand, such as spinach, parsley, lettuce – use your imagination. The most typical ingredients are chilis and cilantro; after that, anything goes. Serious cooks might have time to treat the chilis properly, that is, gently roast them on all sides on a tin surface and steam them in a brown paper bag before peeling them and adding them to the blender.

Dogs' lives are too short. Their only fault, really.
Agnes Sligh Turnbull

DAISY'S MALAY RICE

2 cups cooked rice, white or brown

1 or 2 eggs, beaten

1 T. crushed chilies or red pepper flakes, or to taste

1 tsp. ground coriander

2 T. soy sauce

1 T. sherry

1 T. brown sugar

1 - 2 T. oil

1 onion, chopped

2 - 3 cloves garlic, chopped

1-2 cups chopped vegetables, such as spinach, peas, celery, broccoli rabe, mushrooms, cabbage, red pepper, carrots, or bean sprouts

Add all of the seasonings to the eggs, and reserve. Sauté the onions and garlic briefly in the heated oil, and then add the vegetables, barely cooking them – you want as much tender flavor as possible. Add the beaten eggs, stirring to scramble them into the mixture and put the rice in last, heating it thoroughly before serving. Serves 4-6.

It's a terrible thing for an old woman to outlive her dog.
Tennessee Williams

PILAF CITY

3 cups simmering broth, chicken or vegetable

¼ cup vermicelli (broken into short lengths) or orzo

2 T. oil, butter, or a combination

1½ cups rice, cracked wheat, or quinoa

salt and pepper to taste

optional: ¼ tsp. allspice

optional: chopped onion, garlic, toasted pine nuts, or almonds

In one saucepan, bring the broth to a boil and reserve. In another, over medium heat, sauté the vermicelli in the oil until it turns golden. Add the rice and continue cooking until it glistens and some of the grains have white spots on them. Then add the broth, bring it again to a boil, turn down the heat, cover, and simmer for exactly 20 minutes. Sprinkle it with the allspice, fluff it up, taste for seasoning and serve. For parties, toast ¼ cup of nuts in 1 tsp. butter for a minute or two and sprinkle them on top. Serves 4.

The pilaf lady contributed this recipe because it is so simple to prepare. Sometimes she sautés a little onion or garlic with the vermicelli or orzo, and she often uses pilaf for the base of a meal, topping it with leftover meat and/or sautéed mushrooms or other vegetables; there is no end to its versatility. She told us about finding some giant cracked wheat in a nearby market, which she loved, because she usually uses a medium grain. Quinoa is her newest discovery – it evidently behaves exactly like rice or cracked wheat, but it's loaded with protein. Leftover pilafs are often mixed with a vinaigrette and eaten as a salad with bits of refrigerator surplus, and crisp stuff added, like chopped peppers, scallions, and herbs.

When a cat is aggressive, anger only makes it worse – simply say "No" in a gentle, firm tone and try to distract the cat with a toy.

JANET'S POLENTA PIE

2 cups cold water

2 cups cold milk

1 cup corn meal

8 oz. sour cream

salt and pepper to taste

optional: ½ cup fresh Parmesan cheese, grated

4 - 6 T. blue, soft Brie, or smoked mozzarella cheese in bits

Preheat the oven to 350. Put the cold water and the milk into a medium-sized pan, add the corn meal, and whisk to blend. Turn on the heat, bring to a boil, and cook gently, stirring, for about 5 minutes, until it thickens. Cool. Stir in the sour cream (and the optional Parmesan) and season. Pour the mixture into a 10" round pan or pie plate, and sprinkle one of the cheeses on top. Bake it for 20 minutes and then put it under the broiler for a few minutes to brown before serving. Or bake it for an hour and forget the broiler. Serve this as a rich side dish at dinner, or make it into a fancy lunch, and top it with shrimps that have been sautéed in olive oil with garlic and white wine. Serves 6-8.

If manners maketh man, then manner and grooming maketh poodle.
John Steinbeck

LINEN POLENTA

4 cups broth – two cold, two hot
1 cup corn meal
½ tsp. salt
optional: ½ cup shaved or grated Parmesan cheese
optional: 2 T. olive oil or butter

Pour the cold broth into a small bowl, add the corn meal, and whisk to blend. Meanwhile, in a large, heavy saucepan, heat the rest of the broth and when it boils, whisk in the paste and bring it back to the boil. Cook it slowly over low heat, stirring occasionally, until it becomes shiny, smooth, and thick; 30-40 minutes. You may enrich it by adding, as it cooks, the cheese and/or olive oil. When it is done, with diners sitting at the table, place a large cutting board in the center, covered with a linen towel or cloth. Pour the polenta over the cloth (it will set quickly) and, using a spatula or wooden paddle, cut and scoop portions onto your guests' heated plates. Serve it with your favorite spaghetti sauce. Serves 4.

Italians have for generations served polenta straight out of the pot and onto the tablecloth; this recipe, simple to make, returns that charming custom, and suggests it for your next gathering. (Italians also like to cut it with a string: give it a try!)

Polenta is one of the easiest, most obediently absorbent bases for a meal that we know of. There is no end to its potential once you know the rule. Add herbs, add cheese; or add chopped jalapeño peppers and serve it with salsa. Pour it into an oiled loaf pan, chill it, and slice it – you can then grill, broil, or sauté it. You can sprinkle grated Parmesan on a slice and toast it in the toaster oven, or dip it in sesame seeds before frying. Or sauté garlic and piles of mushrooms in a large pan, adding wine and broth when they soften, plus rosemary, thyme or sage. When they have cooked down, season them with butter and salt and pepper, and serve them over slices of polenta. You are limited only by the contents of your cupboard.

MEAT
·&·
POULTRY

10 Easy and Amusing Garnishes

1   Make a chain out of cucumber, zucchini, or summer squash: core thin slices with a small round cutter, slit each ring, and link up chain.

2   Cut thin strips of cheese (¼"x3") and place them on top of a recipe in a diagonal criss-cross form; good for broiling or baking.

3   Do the same with a quick crêpe made of egg, a bit of water, and sesame oil. Julienne the thin pancake into ½" strips and arrange on top of a dish – perhaps a salad or a stir-fry – in a lattice pattern.

4   Make radish jacks: cut slices, notch each one half way through, and put 2 together at the notches. Make lots and store in ice water.

5   Make a tomato rose: with a sharp paring knife, cut the peel into one long strip and, beginning at the center of the rose, wrap the peel around in spiral fashion, forming the flower.

6   Make a scallion brush: remove 1/8" of the bottom root, cut a 3" section of the scallion and, holding the bottom, cut thin slivers 2" into the other end, turning it as you do, to make a lot. Soak them in ice water and they will curl, forming a brush. (Make short ones and pop them into pitted ripe olives for flowers.)

7   Cut a lemon in half the long way and then, flesh down, make 3 long cuts in each half as if dividing it into 4 equal wedges, but do not cut it all the way through. Use unpeeled cucumber slices, halved, to insert into the wedges – voilá, striped lemons!

8   Use the chopstick cut for potato chrysanthemums to brown with a roast: cut a slice off the bottom of a peeled spud and place it between two chopsticks. Holding the knife horizontal to the cutting board, make as many evenly spaced cuts one way as you can, and then repeat with perpendicular cuts, turning the potato ninety degrees. (The knife hitting the chopsticks will not cut all the way through the potato.) Soak the spuds in cold salted water until you need them; then drain and dry. Use this cut for zucchini and cucumber fans, too.

9   Put the yolk of a hard-boiled egg through a sieve, letting the powder fall onto a piece of wax paper; on another piece, do the same thing to the white. Then decorate with the two colors, using the paper as a pouring tool.

10 Make a chili lily, using tiny red peppers: cut them from their tips almost to their stems in half, quarters, eighths – as many as you can – and let the "petals" flare. Keep fresh in ice water.

NANCY'S LEMONY LAMB SHANKS

5 large lamb shanks, about 4 pounds

2 T. butter

1 lb. mushrooms, quartered

2 lemons, rind grated and juice squeezed

½ cup wine, red or white

1 - 2 T. onion soup mix or 1 bunch scallions in 1" pieces

½ cup parsley, chopped

salt and pepper to taste

optional: 3 wine corks (see below)

Preheat the oven to 250. Sauté shanks in hot butter, turning until they are brown all over. Remove them to a nice, deep casserole and reserve. Preheat the oven to 250. Sauté the mushrooms quickly in the leftover butter, and add the lemon juice and wine to deglaze the pan. Pour this into the casserole and add the rind, onion, parsley, and salt and pepper. Cover tightly and bake – it takes 2-4 hours, unless you use a hotter oven, but the slow oven makes them terribly tender. Check every once in a while for moisture, and add water or broth if necessary. Garnish with parsley or lemon, and serve with rice pilaf or potatoes – or peel and quarter some spuds, and cook them for the last hour in the casserole. (If it's a really big night, add another pound of mushrooms.) Serves 6.

Don't throw those wine corks away! The late chef Felipe Rojas-Lombardi discovered that putting 3 wine corks in a pot of meat lessens its cooking time. Evidently, the enzymes exuding from the cork tenderize the flesh, thereby cutting the cooking time almost in half. (Whoever gets a cork in his dish gets a second helping.)

PERUVIAN LAMB SHANKS

1 bunch fresh cilantro

1 12-oz. bottle Dos Equis or Corona dark beer

3½ lb. lamb shanks, cut into 1" pieces

1½ lb. onions, chopped

1½ lb. tomatoes, chopped

1 tsp. salt

1 tsp. pepper

1 tsp. cumin

1½ tsp. paprika

Save a few springs of the cilantro for garnish; put the rest in a blender with ½ cup of the beer, and puree it into a paste. Combine all the ingredients, including the cilantro, in a large stockpot and cook them, uncovered, for about 35 minutes over medium heat, until the meat is tender. (If you would rather bake it, use a 350 oven and bake for an hour or more.) Garnish the shanks with lime wedges and the reserved cilantro, and serve them with rice. Serves 5.

A dog need not be vicious to protect you. A small, yippy dog is a great burglar alarm.

LAMB AND SPINACH STEW KALAMARAS

1 ½ lb. very fresh spinach, washed and stemmed

4 tsp. coarse salt

2 - 3 T. olive oil or butter

2 onions, chopped

1 ½ lb. lean lamb, cut into 1" cubes

1 ½ cup broth, meat or vegetable

½ tsp. allspice, or to taste

pepper to taste

One or two hours before serving the dish, heap the spinach onto two cookie sheets, sprinkle it with the salt, toss, and leave it to drain. (The salting of spinach removes its water but not its nutrients, and allows its color to remain bright green. On the other hand, if you are pressed for time, use 2 10-oz. packages of frozen spinach, thaw it, squeeze it to drain it, and add it at the very end, to simply heat through.) In a large frying pan, heat part of the oil and sauté the onion until it's soft but not brown. Remove and reserve it. Add the lamb, in two batches if necessary, and brown it quickly on all sides, using the remaining oil. Return the onions, add the broth, allspice, and pepper, and simmer, covered, one hour, until the lamb is tender, adding more stock if necessary. Squeeze out as much water from the spinach as you can, and chop it roughly. Place it on top of the meat and simmer, partially covered, 5 or 10 more minutes, no more, until the spinach is just barely tender and still bright green. Serve it at once; pilaf would be a perfect accompaniment. Serves 4-6.

This is an attempt to replicate an ambrosial dish served at a Greek restaurant in London where Momma does the cooking. It arrives looking like a perfectly ordinary stew, but when one tastes it, one is hooked forever.

Killing or eating a cat in ancient Egypt was punishable by death.

MRS. HO'S TASS KEBAB

2 lb. lean lamb, cut into 2" cubes

1½ lb. small white onions, or large ones, quartered

1 6-oz. can tomato paste

½ tsp. ground allspice

½ tsp. ground cumin

salt and pepper to taste

4 - 5 cups cold broth or water

1½ cups raw rice

Mix everything but the water and the rice and pack it tightly into a bowl. Invert the bowl in a large pot, like a frying pan, and place a heavy weight on top; a large clean round rock would be perfect, or a kettle filled with water. Pour the cold broth or water into the pot, forming a moat. Bring it to the boil, and lower the flame to simmer the dish for 2 hours. When it is done, while the dish is still simmering, use a baster to remove 3 cups of the broth for a delicious rice to accompany the lamb. Simmer the broth with the rice for 20 minutes, and serve them together. (Don't worry if, as soon as you turn the heat off under the lamb, all the rest of the liquid is sucked into the bowl; that's physics, and it all comes out in well the end.) Serves 4.

This simple dish is a knockout, especially if you have a nice round rock for a weight. Follow the directions carefully, and you will have a family treasure.

. . . crookeder than a dog's hind leg. Anon.

LAMB AND BEANS FOR JADE

very good in salsa mixture of tomato

1 T. olive oil

¾ lb. boneless lamb, cut into small pieces

1 large onion, chopped

optional: 1 green bell pepper, seeded and chopped

1 cup tomatoes, coarsely chopped fresh or crushed canned

¼ tsp. ground nutmeg

¼ tsp. ground allspice

¼ tsp. ground black pepper

salt to taste

½ lb. fresh green beans, cut into 2" lengths

In a large frying pan or deep pot, heat the olive oil and brown the lamb on all sides. Add the onion (and pepper if you like) and sauté for a few minutes until brown, using more oil if necessary. Put all but the beans into the pan, cover, and simmer for about 30 minutes, and then lay the beans on top of everything and continue simmering until they are barely crisp-tender – another 10 or 15 minutes. Serve with rice pilaf. Serves 4.

Cleanliness in the cat world is usually a virtue put above godliness.
Carl Van Vechten

MEXICAN MEATBALLS

1½ lb. meat: ½ hamburg, ½ ground turkey, or all one

small bunch fresh mint, chopped fine

¾ cup raw rice

salt and pepper to taste

3 large fresh tomatoes, chopped

1 large onion, chopped

3 canned chipotle chilis, chopped

1 T. achiote spice, ground (Spanish market)

1 cup water

lime and avocado for garnish

Combine the first 4 ingredients, taste for seasoning, and form the mixture into 2" balls. Blend the next five ingredients, and put everything in a saucepan. Simmer for a half hour or more, until the rice in the meat is cooked. Garnish with wedges of lime and chopped avocado. Great with Ricardo's Dirty Green Rice. Serves 4.

There's no man so poor but what he can afford to keep one dog. And I have seen them so poor that they could afford to keep three.
Josh Billings

STEAMED CHINESE MEATBALLS

1 lb. ground turkey, beef, shrimp, or any combination

1 T. cold water

1 egg white

2 T. fresh cilantro, chopped fine

2 T. fresh scallions, chopped fine

optional: 3 1" square pieces of tangerine peel, minced

1 T. soy sauce

1 T. dry sherry

2 tsp. sesame oil

1 tsp. cornstarch

Put the ground meat into a blender or processer, add the water and egg white, and puree to blend. Add the rest of the ingredients, mixing to a paste. Form into small balls, put them on a plate, and steam them for 20-30 minutes. Serve them with a dipping sauce (see Chick Pea Flour Chive Pancake) and rice. For a slightly different slant, these meatballs can also be cooked on a grill or a broiler – they'll need watching and turning, and they'll take less time. Serves 4.

It's fun to make odd steaming broths – you can combine whatever goes with the topic at hand, like slices of ginger, some sherry, a few pepper corns, some lemon peel, soy sauce – all added to the pint or so of steaming water. For steaming scallops wrapped in lettuce leaves, for instance, you can use 5 star anise pods in water. A steamer can be made by balancing the plate or platter on one or two empty cat food cans (remove the tops and bottoms) in a large pot or roasting pan. Someone once told us about fastening a dish towel around the lid to keep liquid from dripping on the food.

BROILED PORK SATAY

1 red bell pepper, seeded and rough chopped

1 small onion, rough chopped

3 cloves garlic, halved lengthwise

3 hot red chilis, seeded and chopped, or ½ tsp. cayenne
   pepper

1 T. sugar

1/3 cup soy sauce

2 T. lemon or lime juice

salt to taste

¾ lb. boneless pork loin, cut into 1" cubes

Place everything except the pork into a blender or processer, and puree, tasting for salt. Transfer it to a bowl, and add the pork, tossing it to blend with the marinade. Leave it for at least 2 hours; more if you wish. When you are ready to cook it, preheat the broiler (or grill – this can be done outdoors, too) and pour off the marinade into a saucepan for heating. Put the pork, as close together as possible, onto four skewers and broil on an oiled tray 4-5" from the flame for about 6 minutes, turning them once. Meanwhile, simmer the sauce while the pork is cooking, reducing it a little, and pass it for dipping when you serve the satay. Rice would be nice. Serves 4.

A couple of bags of frozen peas are handy kept in the freezer for when one's back is a problem – place one behind a sore back when driving the car or watching T.V.

CHICKEN OR RABBIT DIJONNAISE

2 2-lb. chickens, cut up

salt and pepper

¼ cup Dijon mustard

1 tsp. oil

4 T. butter

2 T. flour

1 bottle dry white wine

4 bay leaves

2 T. fresh thyme or rosemary, crushed

Sprinkle the chickens with salt and pepper, and coat them with the mustard. In a large skillet, heat the oil, add 3 T. of the butter, and brown the pieces on all sides over high heat. Remove the meat and reserve it in a warm place. Add the flour and the rest of the butter to the pan and cook, stirring, until it's golden. Pour in 2 cups of the wine and whisk to blend. Add the rest, whisking all the time. Now return the chicken to the pan, adding the bay leaves and thyme, and cover to simmer. Turn the pieces several times and cook until the meat is very tender and falling off the bones, about 1 hour. Taste for seasoning and serve with roast potatoes. Serves 6.

In some less civilized countries, lapin is the traditional meat in this recipe – people do eat it, and with great enthusiasm, so if rabbit is available, join the fanatics and give it a try.

When a cat is "stuck" in a tree, forget about trying to rescue it; it is merely thinking things out. When it is ready, it can and will come down. Remember, it climbed up.

URSULA'S RUBY CHICKEN

1 - 2 T. butter

1 3 lb. broiler, cut in pieces and dredged in flour and salt

1½ cups fresh (or whole canned) cranberries

¼ cup sugar

¼ cup onion, chopped

1 tsp. grated orange peel

¾ cup orange juice

¼ tsp. ground cinnamon

¼ tsp. ground ginger (or ½ tsp. fresh, minced)

Heat the butter in a large skillet that has a cover, and brown the chicken (uncovered). While it is cooking, prepare the sauce by combining the rest of the ingredients in a small saucepan and simmering them for about 15 minutes. Pour the sauce over the chicken, cover the pot, and cook it gently for 35-40 minutes, until the chicken is tender. Serves 4.

This popular dish has been served every Tuesday night at the New Ocean House in Port Clyde for the past ten years.

A cat does not negotiate with the mouse. Robert Massie

HULLY GULLY CHICKEN

1 cup soy sauce

3 garlic cloves, crushed

1 12-oz. can of beer

3 whole boneless chicken breasts

Combine the first 3 ingredients in a large mixing bowl. Add the chicken and marinate for 12 hours or overnight, turning occasionally. Grill over hot charcoal, or broil in a 500 degree oven, basting frequently. Cook until the juices run clear. Serve cold in the summer with salad, or hot in cooler months with rice. Great for a pot luck or tailgate picnic. Serves 4-6.

If a dog jumps at you, give it a quick blow in the stomach with your knee; if it's quick enough, the dog won't know where it came from. Be firm when your dog greets you this way, no matter how glad it is to see you. Command it to sit down, and then praise it lavishly, and reward it with a biscuit. It will get used to receiving all of its affection on the ground, and will not jump on people.

ROAST CHICKEN WITH FRESH HERB PASTE

½ cup fresh tarragon, rosemary, or parsley, chopped fine

2 scallions, white part only, chopped fine

2 cloves garlic, minced

zest of 1 lemon

½ tsp. salt

4 tsp. coarse ground pepper

olive oil to moisten, about 3-4 T.

1 chicken, about 3 lb.

Combine all the ingredients, except the chicken, in a processer or blender or else whisk them together in a bowl; the mixture should have the consistency of a paste. Rub it on the chicken and let it sit while you preheat the oven; or refrigerate it, covered, until you need it. Bake at 325 for 1½ hours or until the juices run clear when the bird is pierced. Serves 4.

This coating is equally delicious on lamb or pork, especially when accompanied by roasted potatoes – maybe the ones mentioned in "10 Easy and Amusing Garnishes" under number 8.

The time to get a puppy is when it is six to ten weeks old; any longer than that with only other dogs for company makes it harder for the puppy to adjust to a human family.

MARINATED CHICKEN WITH WALNUT SAUCE

1 chicken, 2½ lb., cut into pieces

grated rind and juice of 2 large lemons

¼ cup olive oil

4 T. fresh parsley, chopped

½ tsp. sugar

optional: pinch of ground cumin

salt and pepper to taste

4 slices bread, with crusts, torn into pieces

2 large cloves garlic, smashed and chopped roughly

2 T. white wine

4 T. olive oil

1 cup walnuts, toasted and ground

salt and pepper to taste

Combine the first 7 ingredients in a covered container or plastic bag and put them in the refrigerator for at least 4 hours or overnight. When you're ready to cook, turn the broiler (or grill) on low, and broil the chicken pieces, skin side down, covered with the marinade. Cook them for about 20 minutes, and then turn them skin side up and baste them, cooking them for 15 more minutes. Meanwhile, prepare the sauce. Soak the bread in warm water for a few seconds, squeeze it out, and place it in a blender, processer, or bowl. Add the garlic and wine and blend, process, or beat, continuing the action while adding the oil in a thin stream. Last of all, stir in the ground nuts, check the seasoning, and add a little water if the sauce seems too thick. Present the chicken with the sauce on a bed of fluffy rice, garnished with parsley. Serves 4.

Lemons and limes will yield more juice if they are heated first. Use a microwave oven (30 seconds on HIGH) or soak them in very hot water for 1 minute.

LEMON WINGS

zest and juice of 2 lemons

1 onion, rough chopped

2 T. brown sugar

3 large cloves of garlic, halved

1 T. soy sauce

2 tsp. ground coriander

½ tsp. hot pepper flakes

3/4 cup dry sherry

20 chicken wings, about 4 lb., tips cut off

lemon for garnish

In a blender or processer, puree the first 8 ingredients. Pour the mixture into a large non-aluminum pot, bring it to a boil, add the wings, and simmer them uncovered for about 30 minutes, turning occasionally. The sauce should have reduced and the wings become tender. Remove the pot from the heat and allow it to cool a little while you preheat the broiler. Place the wings in a baking pan, close together, and spoon some of the sauce over them. Broil on low for about 3 minutes, browning them completely. Do not turn them. They are fun finger food – serve them with lemon wedges, the extra sauce on the side. If you want a meal of them, add rice. Serves 4.

For a Chinese version, combine with the wings in a large bowl or zip-top plastic bag 5 cloves of garlic, minced, 5 T. hoisin sauce, and up to 1/3 cup of liquid (tea, water, or broth) if the mixture seems too thick. Marinate the wings for at least an hour – or overnight in the refrigerator, if you wish – and bake in a 350 oven on a cookie sheet lined with oiled aluminum foil. They will take about 45 minutes, and should be turned once.

One of the most striking differences between a cat and a lie is that a cat has only nine lives. Mark Twain

CHICKEN ELISOFON

4 T. butter

2 3 lb. broilers, cut up and floured

1 lb. mushrooms, sliced

8 cloves garlic, rough chopped

1 large green pepper, diced

1 large jar (12-oz.) pimentos (or roasted red peppers), diced

2 large (28-oz.) cans tomatoes, drained

2 large onions, diced

½ cup fresh parsley, chopped

1½ pint sour cream, at room temperature

1 T. (heaping) paprika, stirred into the sour cream

Preheat the oven to 350. In a good-sized skillet, brown the chicken pieces in the butter and remove them to a large casserole. Do the same with the mushroom slices, adding the garlic at the last minute. Put them, with the remaining ingredients into the casserole, setting aside one cup of the sour cream to be added to the dish just before serving. Bake it for 1 hour and serve it over rice or noodles. Serves 8-10.

Eliot Elisofon, the famous Life Magazine photographer, lived in Maine on Vinalhaven, and was a passionate cook. This dish, his all-time favorite, was served about 30 years ago at the Waldorf-Astoria Hotel in New York at a dinner party given by Life for its war correspondents. Oscar, famed Waldorf chef, had phoned his good friend Eliot for a recipe, tried it, liked it, and served it!

TURKEY TONNATO — A PARTY DISH

1 turkey breast, about 4 lb., skin on

2 large garlic cloves, peeled and quartered lengthwise

1 2-oz. can flat anchovies

1 medium onion, peeled and quartered

1 medium carrot, cut into 1" pieces

1 stick celery, cut into 1" pieces

5 sprigs fresh parsley

3 bay leaves

1 tsp. dry thyme

5 cups chicken stock

2 cups dry white wine

1 7-oz. can solid tuna in oil

1½ cups homemade mayonnaise

3 T. capers for garnish

With the point of a sharp knife, cut 8 incisions, 1" deep, in the top of the turkey breast. Cut 2 of the anchovies crosswise into 4 pieces each. Insert 1 garlic piece and 1 anchovy piece into each incision. Place the turkey breast, skin side down, in an 8-quart casserole. Add the next eight ingredients, bring to a simmer, and simmer gently for 30 minutes. Remove from heat and let it cool to room temperature. Take the turkey out of the pot, skin it, and remove each side of the breast from the bones in one piece. Reassemble it in roughly the shape of the original breast. Cut the new breast crosswise into thick slices, and arrange them on a platter, overlapping slightly. Mix the tuna and mayonnaise in a blender or processer, and spread it over the turkey. Garnish with the remaining anchovies and the capers, in a diagonal tic-tac-toe design with the capers inside each "square". Chill, covered, until ready to serve. serves 8-12.

That tuna mayonnaise shouldn't be used exclusively on this dish; try it on sliced boiled new potatoes as a salad; with zucchini or sliced tomatoes as a veg; on an English muffin at lunch — it's terribly versatile — especially with an anchovy at its side.

SEAFOOD

10 Handy Impostors and Substitutes

1   Fake bittersweet chocolate: for each square (ounce), mix 3 T. cocoa and 1 T. butter, shortening, or oil

2   Fake eggs: for each one, beat together 1 egg white, 2 ¼ tsp. dry milk, and 2 tsp. canola oil (optional: 1 drop yellow food coloring)

3   More fake eggs, this time for two: put 2 egg whites in a ½ cup measure; fill it to the top with nonfat yogurt

4   Fake cornstarch: for one T., use 2 T. flour

5   Fake sweetened condensed milk: for 1½ cups (or 1 can), mix 1 cup dry milk, ½ cup boiling water, 2/3 cup sugar, and 3 T. melted butter; mix it in the blender and store it in the refrigerator

6   Fake buttermilk: mix 1 tsp. vinegar to 1 cup milk

7   Fake crème fraîche: add 2 T. buttermilk to a pint of heavy cream, shake for a minute, and leave it at room temperature overnight or longer, until it thickens; or mix ½ cup sour cream with 1 cup heavy cream and leave it at room temperature for 4 or 5 hours

8   Fake baking powder: for 1 tsp., mix ¼ tsp. baking soda and ½ tsp. cream of tartar

9   Fake mascarpone: 2 cups heavy cream plus 1 lb. ricotta cheese

10 Fake sour cream: combine ½ lb. low-fat cottage cheese with 1½ T. low-fat milk in a blender until it's smooth

PENOBSCOT BAY SCALLOPS WITH WALNUTS

2 T. butter

½ cup fresh breadcrumbs

¼ cup chopped walnuts

2 T. minced parsley

2 T. minced scallions

2 T. lemon juice

1 lb. scallops, cut in half if large

salt and pepper to taste

Preheat the oven to 425. While it is warming, put the butter, crumbs and nuts in an ovenproof pan and heat it in the oven until the butter has melted, stirring and watching it carefully. Add the rest of the ingredients and put the mixture into individual scallop shells or a casserole and bake for about 5 minutes, until the scallops are done. You may pop the dish under the broiler very briefly to brown, if you wish. Lovely with rice. Serves 4.

A dog or horse when admonished becomes submissive — a cat strikes back.

LINCOLNVILLE LOAF

1 cup rye bread, torn into small pieces

1 cup hot milk

2 cups white-fleshed fish, cooked

½ cup celery, diced

2 scallions, chopped fine

½ red or green pepper, diced

½ lemon rind, grated

2 eggs, beaten

2 T. butter, melted

salt to taste

Preheat the oven to 350. In a large bowl, soak the bread in the milk for 5 minutes; add the remaining ingredients and mix well. Pour it into a greased 4-cup loaf pan and bake it for 45 minutes. Serve with your favorite tomato sauce, ketchup, or Frances's Sauce (under Cushing Crab Cakes). Serves 4.

Anything as large as a bloodhound or a golden retriever . . . makes a grand hot water bottle. Roger Caras

CASCO BAY CLAMBURGERS

1 pint chopped clams, drained, the juice saved

1½ cups crumbs, any kind

2 T. flour

2 eggs, whisked lightly

salt and pepper to taste

optional: lemon juice, minced scallions, or parsley

butter for frying

Mix everything but the butter in a bowl, adding clam juice if the batter is too stiff. Drop it by large spoonfuls onto a heated, buttered skillet, pressing to make flat cakes, and turning them after about 3 minutes to brown the other side. Serve them with ketchup. Serves 4.

It takes a great deal of physical courage to ride a horse. This, however, I have. I get it at about forty cents a flask, and take it as required. Stephen Leacock

BAKED CLAM PUFFS

8 oz. minced clams, canned or fresh

1 cup clam broth

1/8 tsp. cayenne pepper

1 or 2 bay leaves, crushed

1 or 2 sage leaves, crushed

½ tsp. fresh marjoram, chopped

1 small onion, chopped fine

1 stalk celery, chopped fine

1 cup flour

½ tsp. salt

½ tsp. Tabasco

4 eggs

Combine the first 8 ingredients in a small saucepan, bring them to a boil, simmer 5 minutes, and strain and cool the juice, reserving the clam mix. Preheat the oven to 450. Put the cooled broth in a larger saucepan and whisk in the flour and the Tabasco. Over low heat, cook it, stirring constantly until it thickens. Remove from the heat and add the eggs, one at a time, beating to incorporate each one. Return to the heat and continue stirring until the mixture becomes very thick. Quickly fold in the clams. Drop the batter by tablespoons onto a baking sheet that has been sprayed with cooking oil and bake for 8 minutes, then lower the heat to 350 and bake for 10 more minutes or until golden brown and puffy. If you make tiny ones, they're great for appetizers – at any rate, serve them with the regulation ketchup and Tabasco, or with Auntie Ruth's Way Hot Chili Sauce or Frances's Sauce. Serves 4.

Ever consider what they think of us? I mean, here we come back from the grocery store with the most amazing haul – chicken, pork, half a cow...they must think we're the greatest hunters on earth!
Anne Tyler

Vinalhaven:

¼ cup melted butter

3 T. olive oil

2 large cloves garlic, minced

2 T. Worcestershire sauce

1 T. Tabasco, or hot sauce if less heat is desired

salt and cracked black pepper to taste

about 1 ½ lb. shrimp in their shells, rinsed and dried

North Haven:

¼ cup olive oil

¼ cup balsamic vinegar

2 cloves garlic, minced

1 T. grated lemon rind

1 T. dry vermouth

2 sprigs fresh rosemary, chopped

salt and cracked black pepper to taste

about 1 ½ lb. shrimp in their shells, rinsed and dried

Combine all of the ingredients in a bowl or a seal-top plastic bag and marinate them at room temperature for about 45 minutes, squeezing the bag once or twice to mix the contents. (You may also do this the night before, marinating them in the refrigerator and removing the bag an hour before cooking time.) The Vinalhaven version will seem too thick; that's normal. Meanwhile, heat the broiler, the grill, or a large black skillet, and cook the shrimp quickly, turning them often, and using as much of the marinade as you can. Serve them on a heated platter, with lots of paper napkins nearby and plenty of beer. Some folks like to eat them in their crispy shells; others prefer to peel them. Each serves 4-6.

It is not safe to leave a small child alone with even the gentlest of dogs.

CUSHING CRAB CAKES

½ cup fresh bread crumbs

1 egg, beaten

2 T. mayonnaise

1 tsp. Worcestershire sauce

few drops Tabasco sauce

3 T. chives, chopped

1 T. fresh parsley, chopped fine

1/8 tsp. salt

8 oz. fresh Maine crabmeat

½ cup fresh bread crumbs for dredging

2 T. butter

Combine all the ingredients except the last 2, adding the crabmeat at the end and folding it in gently to keep the pieces as whole as possible. Form the mixture into 6 balls, and flatten them into ½" cakes. Put them on wax paper on a plate in the refrigerator to chill while you make the sauce, and then, dredging them in the bread crumbs, brown them on both sides in the butter – about 2 minutes for each side. Serve them on warmed plates with their sauce. Makes 6 cakes.

FRANCES'S SAUCE

1/2 cup mayonnaise

1/3 cup plain yogurt

1 T. lemon juice, or to taste

3 T. Spanish olives, chopped

1 T. capers, chopped

1/8 tsp. salt

Combine all the ingredients and blend them thoroughly. Use this sauce on crab cakes, fish cakes, and cold fish, or wherever you might like tartar sauce.

SMOKE YOUR OWN MUSSELS, ORIENTAL STYLE

2 cloves of garlic, smashed

1 tsp. fresh thyme or 2 bay leaves, crushed

¼ cup dry white wine

2 T. olive oil

2 lb. cultured mussels, (preferably Great Eastern), de-bearded

2 T. flour

2 T. sugar

2 T. tea leaves, any kind

olive oil and balsamic vinegar for sprinkling

In a large kettle, combine the first 4 ingredients, bring them to a boil, put in the mussels, cover, and cook them until they open, about 4-5 minutes. Remove them at once and reserve. Meanwhile, put a sheet of aluminum foil in the bottom of a large pot, combine the flour, sugar, and tea, and place them on the foil. Lay an old empty cat food can with its ends removed in the center of it all, and put a plate on it. Cover the pot, turn on the heat, and wait for smoke to puff out of the lid. While you are waiting, remove the top shells of all the mussels, and, when smoke appears, put them on the plate in the pot. Cover it, turn the heat on high until smoke appears again, and then turn it down and smoke the mussels for 5-8 minutes: they'll look dark. Serve them sprinkled with a mixture of 2 T. oil and 1 T. vinegar, and pass the French bread and wine. Serves 4

This sounds like a crazy recipe, but it's terribly easy, it's fast, and it's festive. Mussel lovers will be surprised at the entirely new flavor it gives to their favorite mollusk.

There are no ordinary cats. Colette

MUSSELS LION'S MAINE, MERCI JACQUES PÉPIN

4 lb. fresh mussels steamed in wine, herbs and olive oil

2 T. butter

2 T. flour

½ cup light cream or half-and-half

3 cups fragrant cooked rice, pilaf if possible, kept hot

When the mussels have opened in their broth, put them at once into a colander, saving their liquid; remove them from their shells, and set aside the meats. Strain the broth through a coffee filter and reserve it. Melt the butter into a small saucepan, stir in the flour and slowly add 1½ cups of the broth, whisking it to blend. Bring the sauce to a boil, continuing to whisk it, and let it simmer for a minute before adding the cream. Simmer it for another minute or two to thicken it, and remove it from the stove. For each serving, generously butter the inside of a small round cup and put in a few spoonfuls of the rice, lining the bottom and sides to form a nest. Place a few mussels in it, add a bit of sauce, and pack in more rice, filling the cup. Place a small serving plate over it, invert, and let the rice out. Puddle a bit more of the sauce around it, garnish with a sprig of something, and serve as soon as possible. (It can also be made in one large bowl, and served at the table.) Serves 6.

There's a fascinating picnic way of serving mussels in France called l'éclade, in which the mollusks are packed on a wet wooden board in a star pattern, starting from the center, hinges down, tightly together so they can't open, and covered with a thick layer of dry pine needles. The needles are lighted and their flames cook the mussels, which only need a few minutes because of their thin shells. The ashes are fanned off, the melted butter is passed, and the feasting begins.

SIMPLE SALMON: THE COOK-OFF WINNER

1½ lb. fresh salmon steaks (enough for 4 servings)
your favorite barbecue sauce

Coat the salmon pieces with the sauce and put them on the grill, about 5 inches from the source of the heat, cooking them 4 minutes on one side and a bit less on the other – a total of 7-8 minutes if they are ¾" thick (the rule being 10 minutes per inch of thickness). The pieces should flake easily on the edges when they are done. There are many variations of sauce: for instance, Kentucky denizens may blanch, but try adding ¼ cup of bourbon to each cup of barbecue sauce. Or go the satay route by whisking into 1 cup of barbecue sauce 1/3 cup smooth peanut butter, 2 tsp. sesame oil, and 3 T. soy sauce. The choice is yours – barbecue sauce cook-off next week! Serves 4.

If you have a new baby in the house, and there is a cat or dog in residence, be sure to make time for it every day so that it knows it hasn't been replaced in your affection.

SALMON ON A STICK

1 lb. fresh salmon, cut into chunks for broiling

3 T. dry sherry or vermouth

4 oz. butter

juice of 2 lemons

½ lb. small onions, peeled, or 4 large ones, quartered

10 oz. mushrooms

16 bay leaves

Marinate the salmon for an hour or so in the sherry, turning it occasionally. Preheat the broiler and prepare a foil-lined pan with a rack (or light the grill). Put the butter and lemon juice in a pan, and melt them together. Thread skewers with alternating ingredients, placing the bay leaves at each end, and anywhere in the middle. Brush the butter mix liberally over the skewers, and broil, continuing to baste, until the fish is cooked. Mix the pan juices with the rest of the butter, and serve on the side. Serves 4.

If you get a new kitten a scratching post right away, it will save your furniture. It should be tall and sturdy, and can be covered with carpeting. Show the kitten how to use it by holding his paws and scratching them on the post.

FISH IN A MUSTARD-COLORED COAT

Excellent on Haddock (handwritten)

¼ cup Dijon mustard
3 T. balsamic or cider vinegar
2 T. brown sugar
1 tsp. freshly cracked black pepper
4 cod (or any firm fish) fillets, 6-8 oz. each
1 cup fresh black bread crumbs (pumpernickel or rye) *tiny crumbs* (handwritten)
optional: melted butter for drizzling

Preheat the oven to 400. Combine the mustard, vinegar, sugar, and pepper in a small bowl. Lay the fillets on a lightly oiled baking sheet and cover each one with a quarter of the mustard combination. Top with the bread crumbs, (drizzle with the butter) and bake for 8-10 minutes, until the fish is tender and moist. Serves 4.

When you are teaching children how to approach a dog, tell them to make a fist and let the dog sniff it before they pet the dog.

10 MINUTE POACHED FISH WITH LEMON & BASIL

¼ cup strong broth: fish or chicken

2 T. olive oil

3 T. lemon juice

1 lb. fresh sole or any tender white fish fillets

2 T. fresh basil or cilantro, chopped

1 T. lemon peel, minced, or zest

In a large skillet, simmer the first 3 ingredients for 5 minutes. Turn off the heat and gently slip the fillets into the liquid (if necessary, folding tails under) and scatter the basil over all. Cover the pan and simmer until the fish is opaque but almost translucent in the thickest part (cut and peek), about 2 minutes (longer if thicker than fillet of sole). Place the fish on warmed serving plates while you reduce the sauce in the pan to about ¼ cup, about 3 minutes. Dribble it over the fish and scatter the lemon peel on top. Serves 4.

"Milk" for the lactose intolerant can be made with nuts and seeds — cashews, almonds, sunflower and sesame seeds, for example. Put a cup of them in a blender with an equal amount of water and a pinch of salt and blend at a low speed, adding more water as the stuff thickens, and increasing the speed of the blender until the mixture is creamy. Strain it and keep it in the refrigerator. It's wonderful poured over cereals.

FISH IN GRAPE LEAVES

1 lb. fish: salmon, whitefish, etc., cut into 2" pieces

1 bunch scallions, green part, slivered

½ lemon, thin sliced

1 small jar grape leaves (or pick your own)

1-2 cups dry white wine

Preheat the oven to 350. Wrap the fish pieces in leaves, including some scallion, and arrange them in a glass baking dish. On top of each roll, place ¼ of a lemon slice, and pour in wine to come part way up the fish, not to cover. Bake for 20 minutes, uncovered, and serve. It would be nice with rice pilaf. Serves 4-6.

Grape leaves are simple: snip off the stem, put the leaf smooth side down, and place the filling in the center; turn in the sides, and roll up. Put the rolls seam side down in the baking dish. They are also very well behaved on the grill, as is this recipe – just brush a little oil on first.

When embarrassed, a cat may stop and groom itself. Scientists call this displacement activity.

5 MINUTE LEMON FISH FILLETS IN THE MICROWAVE

4 fillets of sole or tender white fish, 1-1½ lb.

garlic salt and lemon pepper to taste

½ cup dry white wine or dry vermouth

1 T. fresh lemon juice

long strips of lemon zest, fresh parsley, or dill for garnish

For each of the 4 portions of fish, place two connected paper towels on the counter, and put the piece of fish across the center perforations. Season each one with the salt and pepper, and fold the long sides of the towel towards the center, then fold both open ends toward the center, overlapping on the fish. Place the packets on a microwave safe platter, perforated side up to vent, with the thickest parts of the fillets toward the edges of the platter. Douse with the wine. Cover with an additional damp towel, and microwave on HIGH for 5-7 minutes, rotating the plate once. Let stand for 1 minute and serve splashed with lemon juice and garnished with the zest, parsley, or dill. Serves 4.

A variation of this is to marinate the fish for an hour in a glass dish in a mixture of 1/3 cup wine, ¼ tsp. salt, 2 scallions cut into 1" pieces, and 6 thin slices of fresh ginger. Turn it a couple of times to be sure the marinade is evenly distributed. Remove it from the liquid and microwave as above, sprinkling the paper towels with the marinade. Just before serving, put ¼ cup of sesame oil into a small saucepan, and heat it until it begins to smoke. Put the fish on a platter with a pile of chopped scallions on top and pour on the sesame oil and sprinkle the fish with soy sauce. It will make a very satisfying crackling sound, the audience will applaud, and you will take a bow.

Cats cool themselves by licking their fur and panting.

ONE-DISH MEALS

10 Killer Pizza Toppings – After the Tomato Sauce and/or Cheese

1   Sliced boiled potatoes drizzled with olive oil, caramelized onions, rosemary, and garlic.

2   Wedges of various pestos divided by strips of pepper, anchovies, or asparagus spears.

3   Broiled or grilled eggplant slices smeared with tapenade and scattered with mushroom slices.

4   Alternating wedges of chopped grilled or roasted red peppers and Greek olives divided by anchovy strips and sprinkled with parsley.

5   Thin sliced yellow tomatoes with slivered garlic and basil – sprinkled after baking with borage blossoms?

6   Chopped canned clams, slivered garlic, parsley, or cilantro, and olive oil.

7   3-Tomato Topping: Tomato sauce, cheese, thin sliced fresh tomatoes, sprinkled with pieces of sun-dried tomatoes and fresh basil.

8   Smoked mozzarella, smoked mussels, lemon juice, and parsley.

9   Steve's Favorite: slices of large Spanish olives on top of slices of chorizo.

10 Tomato sauce and/or salsa, pepper jack cheese, chopped chilis, black olives, garlic, and cilantro. Topped when cooked with sour cream and avocado slices.

ASPARAGUS TART TENANTS HARBOR

1 sheet frozen puff pastry, thawed, or your favorite pie crust

1 T. butter

½ lb. mushrooms, sliced

1 lb. asparagus, cut diagonally into 2" pieces

4 eggs, beaten

1 cup milk

2 T. chives, parsley, or tarragon, or a combination

salt and pepper to taste

4-6 oz. feta cheese, crumbled

Preheat the oven to 400. Roll out the pastry into a size large enough to fill and overflow a 10" tart pan, preferably one with a removable bottom. Fit the dough into and up the sides of the pan, using a rolling pin to trim the crust evenly. Refrigerate it while you make the filling (the longer the better if it's puff pastry). Sauté the mushrooms quickly in the butter and steam or blanch the asparagus briefly if at all – they will both cook in the tart. Combine the next 4 ingredients, and assemble the tart by putting the vegetables in first, gently pouring the egg mixture over them, and sprinkling the cheese on top. Bake it for 15 minutes and then reduce the oven to 350 and bake the tart for 10 more minutes; by then it should be set. If you like the idea of individual tarts, do it, by all means! Serves 6.

There's a painter on Monhegan Island who is also known for the tea sandwiches she brings to the annual artists' beach party. She cuts out rounds of very fresh, thin-sliced bread and spreads half of them with a mixture of smoked salmon, dill, and cream cheese. Her secret is that she embosses the top halves by pressing the bottom of her cut glass salt shaker into each one, making quite the most elegant sandwiches we have ever heard of.

KUFTE (ARMENIAN MEAT BALLS) IN TOMATO JUICE

1 lb. ground lamb or beef (or half and half)

1 egg

½ cup bread crumbs

1 large clove garlic, minced

½ tsp. allspice

salt and pepper to taste

1 - 2 T. butter

1 qt. (more or less) tomato juice

optional: chopped parsley for garnish

Mix together all the ingredients except for the butter and the tomato juice and form the meat into small balls. Brown them in the butter in a large frying pan, and then pour the tomato juice over them. Simmer for 30 minutes and serve them with rice pilaf. The first time you taste this, you will not believe how simple it is to produce such a complicated flavor. Serves 4.

If there is one spot of sun spilling onto the floor, a cat will find it and soak it up. Joan McIntosh

PEKING NOODLES WITH GROUND PORK OR TURKEY

½ cup sweet bean paste (Chinese market)

2 T. soy sauce

1½ T. hoisin sauce (Chinese market)

½ lb. ground pork or turkey

2 T. dry sherry

broth or oil for frying

½ cup scallions, chopped

1 T. cornstarch in 2 T. of cold water

12 oz. vermicelli, cooked, drained, and kept warm

¼ lb. fresh bean sprouts

extra scallions for garnish

Combine the bean paste, soy sauce and hoisin in a small bowl and reserve. Meanwhile, mix the pork and the sherry together, heat the optional oil in a skillet or wok, and fry the meat quickly. Add the scallions, cook them for a minute, and then add the bean paste mixture and 1 cup of water. Simmer for a few minutes, and then thicken it with the cornstarch. Combine the meat mixture with the vermicelli, top with the bean sprouts, garnish, and serve. And try not to look too pleased with yourself at how easy this was to fix! Serves 4.

How to make your own raisins: Go to the store. Buy a bunch of seedless grapes. Take it home and put it on a plate. Leave it for a month or two. Voilá! Raisins! (Or better, marry a still life painter.)

FRIENDSHIP FRITTATA

1 cup cooked fish, cut into 1" pieces

½ cup cooked lobster, cut into 1" pieces

¼ cup parsley, chopped

¼ cup flavored breadcrumbs

1 tsp. grated lemon peel

6 eggs, beaten lightly

2 T. milk

½ tsp. salt

2 T. butter

¼ cup cheese, shredded

Combine the first 5 ingredients in a bowl and set it aside. Put the eggs in a separate bowl, whisk in the milk and the salt, and reserve. Heat the butter in a large iron skillet, and at the same time turn on the broiler. Stir the egg mixture into the fish, and put all of it into the skillet, tilting it and lifting the edges with a fork so that the egg covers the bottom. When it begins to set, sprinkle the cheese on top and place it under the broiler. As soon as the cheese melts and the top is set, it is ready to serve. Serves 4.

Any combination of cooked seafood is good in this dish, as is canned crabmeat, smoked salmon, and even sea legs. Feel free to add herbs or spice – anything that you love with seafood.

Authors like cats because they are such quiet, lovable, wise creatures, and cats like authors for the same reasons.
Robertson Davies

FINGERS OF FIRE FRITTATA

1 large egg and 3 large egg whites

salt and pepper to taste

1 7-oz. can sliced jalapeño peppers, drained (1 cup)

1 10-oz. pkg. frozen corn, thawed, or kernels from 4 cobs

3 T. olive oil

2 red or green bell peppers, seeded and rough chopped

1 large onion, rough chopped

4 large cloves garlic, sliced

4 oz. (1 cup) shredded pepper jack or sharp cheddar cheese

optional: fresh cilantro

Whisk the eggs, salt and pepper, and 4 T. of the optional cilantro together in a bowl until frothy and blended, stir in the jalapeños and corn, and reserve. In a medium-sized black iron skillet, heat the oil and quickly sauté the next 3 ingredients over high heat until fragrant and tender, adding the garlic at the last minute. Pour in the egg mixture and stir to combine. Turn the heat down, cook the eggs for a minute or two, and as soon as they have begun to set, pierce them with a fork and tilt the pan to let any extra liquid seep to the bottom. Cover the pan and cook until set, about 5 more minutes. Meanwhile, preheat the broiler (on low if you can). When the eggs are almost set, but still slightly moist, add the cheese and place under the broiler, at least 4" away from the heat; cook until the frittata is brown on top. Serve at once, garnished with cilantro leaves. Serves 6.

The safe way to avoid a dogfight is to prevent it by leashing your dog in public. If you sense signs of aggression towards another dog, like a stiffening, or rising backles, say "No" and move away quickly.

MEDITERRANEAN STRATA

2 eggs, beaten

1½ cup milk, warmed

salt, pepper, and garlic to taste

½ loaf sourdough bread, cut into cubes

2 pkgs. (10-oz.) frozen chopped spinach, thawed and squeezed

1/3 cup fresh basil, chopped

½ cup sun-dried tomatoes (in oil, drained, or dried and
      rehydrated), chopped

2½ cups mozzarella or pepper jack, shredded (save 1 cup for
      top)

Preheat the oven to 350. Combine the first 3 ingredients and add the bread to the mixture to soak until it's soft – about 2 minutes. Divide it in half. Put one half into a greased casserole and layer the spinach, basil, tomatoes, and cheese on top, adding the last half of the bread mix and topping it with the cheese. Bake for 40-45 minutes. This dish can be prepared ahead of time and kept in the refrigerator to be baked later, if you wish. Serves 6.

Stale bread alert! Puddings are some of the most versatile dishes there are. Anything stale in the bread family is fair game: corn bread or muffins, rolls, even pumpernickel. (And of course, stale or unsuccessful cake or sweet rolls are perfect for dessert dishes.) Using the rule for strata, above, the cupboard can be your palette. Just divide the bread part into halves or thirds, depending on how many ingredients there are. Crabmeat, chorizo sausage, olives, artichokes, asparagus, mushrooms, leftovers – create your own one-dish meal. Toppings can include bacon bits, crushed taco chips, canned French-fried onion rings, crushed cereals, red pepper flakes, etc. Liquids can be broths, or warmed low-fat-yogurt- plus-salsa, if Tex-Mex is one of your favorites. (Serve it with hot pepper jelly.) You can cook these dishes in the microwave to save time, and brown them quickly under the broiler. They can be made in winter squash halves, cooking the squash first for 10 minutes in the microwave – there is no end. . .

CABBAGE (BREAD) PUDDING

1 cabbage, about 2 lb., cored and shredded

3 slices stale bread, cut into 1" pieces

8 oz. cheddar cheese, shredded

1 ½ cup milk

2 eggs

1 - 2 T. Dijon mustard

salt to taste

optional: grated Parmesan cheese for dusting

Preheat the oven to 350. Prepare a 2-quart baking dish by oiling it and (optional) dusting the inside with grated Parmesan. Blanch the cabbage (there should be about 4 cups) in boiling water until just barely tender. Drain at once, and put half of it into the baking dish. Combine the bread and the cheese in a separate small bowl, or use a processer and then put the mix in a small bowl. In another bowl, beat the milk, eggs, mustard, and salt together and reserve. Spread half the bread mixture over the cabbage in the baking dish, put the rest of the cabbage over it, and top with the remaining bread mixture. Carefully pour the egg mix into the casserole and press down gently. Let it rest for about 20 minutes, and bake it for 30 minutes. Serves 6-8.

This is another recipe that delighted us with its odd and wonderful flavor, especially because cabbage is always in season.

Anybody who doesn't know what soap tastes like never washed a dog. Franklin P. Jones

DEB'S PARTY PUDDING PRIMAVERA

15 thick slices stale bread, torn into large pieces

3 cups warm milk

1 lb. fresh asparagus, cut into 2" diagonals

4 oz. feta cheese, crumbled

4 oz. cheddar cheese, shredded

½ cup Parmesan cheese, freshly grated – reserve 2 T.

5 eggs, beaten

½ cup fresh herbs, mixed: parsley, chives, tarragon, thyme, etc., chopped

salt and pepper to taste

1 T. butter to dot on top of casserole

Preheat the oven to 350. Soak the bread in the milk to soften for about 2 minutes and squeeze out the milk, saving it. Have a pot of boiling water ready, and pop the asparagus in for exactly 1 minute. Drain it, refresh it under cold water, and set aside about 8 pieces for a garnish. Combine the next 2 cheeses in a bowl and reserve. In another bowl, mix together the milk, the Parmesan cheese, the eggs, herbs, and salt and pepper. Butter and sprinkle with the reserved Parmesan a 3-quart ovenproof casserole. Put 1/3 of the bread into the casserole and top with half the asparagus. Sprinkle with 1/3 of the cheese mix and repeat, using half of the remaining bread, all of the greens, and half of the rest of the cheese. Put the last of the bread on top, sprinkle with the cheese, and garnish with the extra asparagus. Pour the egg-and-milk mix over it all and dot with the butter. Bake the pudding for about 45 minutes, until the top is lightly browned and a knife inserted in the middle comes out clean. Serves 6-8.

When asparagus is cheap, blanch it quickly and freeze the spears for later use. Do not defrost them before cooking – they become tough, so keep them frozen until the last minute.

GUADALAJARA TORTILLA LASAGNE

3 poached chicken breast halves, chopped or shredded
   or 1½ lb. ground turkey, sautéed in butter and crumbled
½ tsp. coarse salt
¼ tsp. black pepper
¼ lb. sharp cheddar cheese, shredded
½ lb. pepper or plain monterey jack cheese, shredded
1 medium onion, chopped
3 large cloves garlic, chopped
1 cup canned jalapeño peppers
4 cups canned tomatillos
1 cup milk or yogurt
2 cups sour cream
1 pkg. 18 6" corn tortillas, about 10 oz.
½ cup ripe olives, pitted and rough chopped
optional: fresh cilantro for garnish

In one bowl, place the chicken and toss it with the salt and pepper. In another, blend the two cheeses. In a blender or a processer, pulse the onion, garlic, jalapeños and tomatillos to a rough chop, and put them in a third bowl. Combine the milk and sour cream in another bowl. Preheat the oven to 350. In a 9x12 lasagne pan, drizzle a thin layer of the green sauce on the bottom, add a layer of 6 tortillas, and sprinkle half of the chicken on top. Drizzle a third of the remaining green sauce over this, add half the cheese and one third of the sour cream mix. Add another layer of tortillas, the rest of the chicken, half of the green sauce, half of the cheese, half of the sour cream and all the rest of the tortillas. Now use up the remaining green sauce, sour cream, and cheese in that order, and sprinkle the olives over everything. Bake the lasagne for about 35 minutes, uncovered, until the cheese melts and the dish is hot and fragrant. Serves 8-10.

You need a navigator for this casserole, but it'll be worth it to hire one – we wouldn't have included it otherwise.

DAY'S COUSCOUS CASSEROLE FOR A PARTY

2 qts. chicken stock
½ cup olive oil
1 T. turmeric
1 T. ground cinnamon
1 T. ground ginger

1 17-oz. pkg. instant couscous
1 cup golden raisins
1 cup pitted dates, diced

1 large summer squash, cut into ¼" dice
1 large zucchini, cut into ¼" dice
6 carrots, cut into ¼" dice
1 large red onion, chopped
3 ripe medium tomatoes, cut into ¼" dice
2 cups chick peas, cooked or canned
1 cup slivered almonds, slightly toasted

1 cup olive oil
½ cup lemon juice
¼-½ tsp. salt

Combine the first five ingredients in a large saucepan. Heat to a full boil and add the couscous. Cook until most of the liquid is absorbed, about 2 minutes. Remove from the heat and stir in the raisins and dates. Cover the pot tightly and let it stand undisturbed for 15 minutes. Meanwhile, combine the next seven ingredients in a large mixing bowl. Whisk the oil and lemon juice together and pour them over the salad, tossing to coat. Add the couscous and stir to blend. Season with salt. Serve this slightly chilled or at room temperature; it will keep in the refrigerator for a week. Serves 15-20.

File this one under Worth the Trouble, because the only time it takes is assembling the ingredients – after that it's clear sailing, and lots of telephone calls the next day.

SAUCES

10 Considerations for the Well-Equipped Larder: a Quirky List

1   Fresh lemons, garlic, parsley, and ginger

2   Greek olives

3   Sun-dried tomatoes

4   Adobo spice (in Spanish section of the market)

5   Anchovies/anchovy paste

6   Smoked mozzarella or other smoked cheese

7   Walnuts or pecans, almonds, and pine nuts (pignoli)

8   Red pepper flakes and bacon bits

9   A block of fresh Parmesan cheese

10 Dried mushrooms

PESTO POMODORO – "RED PESTO"

12-15 sun-dried tomatoes, rough chopped

1 2-oz. can rolled anchovies with capers and oil

2 large cloves garlic, slivered

2 T. fresh basil, rough chopped

1/3 cup red wine

extra olive oil if necessary

fresh Parmesan cheese, shaved, for garnish

optional: pine nuts, toasted, and/or fresh basil for garnish

If the tomatoes are dry, simmer them in a cup of water for 5 minutes and drain before chopping; if in oil, simply drain them. Pour the anchovy oil into a small skillet, reserving the anchovies. Add the garlic and sauté it for a minute. Add the tomatoes, basil, and anchovies and cook over low heat for 10 minutes, mashing the anchovies as you do. For the last 3 minutes of cooking, splash in the wine. Then remove it from the stove and whir it in a blender or processer, adding more oil if it seems too thick (it will). Serve it on hot pasta, sprinkling with fresh Parmesan shavings and garnishing with your favorite decor. This pesto can be saved in a jar in the refrigerator for months if a thin layer of olive oil is floated on top. (In fact, because one cup is never enough, better double this recipe if you have enough of the ingredients.) Makes 1 cup.

Save a dozen of the driest sun-dried tomatoes in the batch, and snip them into pieces that your blender or small processor will accept. Turn them into flakes that can be stored in a covered container and used later on salads, soups, pastas, and casseroles for a fast-flavored garnish.

TAPENADE, OR BLACK OLIVE PESTO

½ lb. French (Niçoise) olives or Greek Kalamatas, pitted

6 anchovy fillets, drained

2-4 large cloves garlic

1½ T. capers

½ tsp. dried thyme, or 1 tsp. fresh, chopped

½ tsp. dried rosemary, or 1 tsp. fresh, chopped

1 tsp. Dijon mustard

1 T. lemon juice

2 T. olive oil

optional: 2 T. cognac

Pulverize all the ingredients in a processer or blender. If the pesto is too salty, add ½ tsp. sugar and a little more oil. Use it in mushroom caps, on grilled eggplant, on cold pasta, or with hard boiled eggs. Makes about 2 cups.

SUN-DRIED TOMATO TAPENADE

1/3 cup olive oil

8 whole garlic cloves, peeled

12 Greek olives, pitted and chopped

3 T. sun-dried tomatoes in oil, chopped

1 cup fresh basil leaves, rough chopped

1 T. capers

Heat the olive oil in a skillet and cook the garlic very slowly until it becomes soft and golden. In a processer or blender, puree the olives, tomatoes, and basil for a second or two, and then add the garlic and olive oil and process briefly: leave a little texture. Stir the capers in whole, put the mixture into a crock, and keep it in the refrigerator. Makes about 1 cup.

WALNUT PESTO

1 cup walnuts, toasted

2 cloves garlic, minced, or to taste

2 T. fresh parsley, minced

4 oz. cream cheese in pieces, or ½ cup ricotta

¼ tsp. salt

4 T. olive oil

warm broth, milk, or water for thinning

cracked black pepper or minced parsley for garnish

Put everything but the liquids into a blender or processer and blend quickly, for about 10 seconds. Add the oil in a thin stream, combining it to form a paste. Thin it to the desired consistency if you're using it on pasta. Makes about 2 cups.

This pesto makes a terrific spaghetti sauce, with or without shredded poached chicken breast or leftover fish – and it tastes wonderful with cracked pepper. A friend tossed some fresh cut green beans into a pot with some penne boiling in it, drained them both at once, and served them in bowls with dollops of the thinned pesto on top – delicious, and really fast. Serve some of it (not thinned out) on top of an 8-oz. portion of Neufchatel cheese, sprinkled with pepper or parsley – or both – as a last-minute appetizer with crackers. And try it on potato salad, thinned.

Cats will always lie soft. Theocritus

ANCHOÏADE: PESTO FOR ANCHOVY LOVERS

3 slices bread, crusts removed
¼ cup warm milk
24 anchovy fillets
2 garlic cloves, minced
½ tsp. black peppercorns, cracked
1 cup or less olive oil

In a small bowl, pour the milk over the bread, let it sit for a minute, then squeeze the liquid out and put the bread aside. Put the anchovies in a mortar, bowl, or blender and mash or puree them, adding the garlic and cracked pepper and blending. Then add the wet bread, and begin to drizzle the olive oil into the mixture (beating it with a fork if you do not have a blender); continue blending until it becomes a smooth sauce. Makes about 1 cup.

This is a lovely way to complement fresh raw vegetables, and it can be made into a bagna cauda by heating it gently in a pan with a little melted butter. Served warm, it lavishes leftovers.

If dogs and children had money, sausage and candy would be the dearest things in the world. Italian proverb

SKORDALIA: GARLIC SAUCE FOR EVERYTHING

10 slices bread, torn into pieces, or 2 cups mashed potatoes

6 - 8 cloves garlic

1 egg

½ cup pignoli nuts or blanched almonds, toasted

2 T. lemon juice

2 T. chopped fresh parsley

½ tsp. salt; pepper to taste

½ cup olive oil

Soak the bread (with or without crusts – it doesn't matter) in warm water for a minute to soften, put it into a sieve, and press it to squeeze it dry. Put all but the oil into a processer or blender and puree for about 10 seconds to mix them. Then add the olive oil in a thin stream until the sauce is of a mayonnaise-like density. Makes 2-3 cups.

Often used for warm or cold poached fish, there's nothing that this sauce doesn't love. Pretend it's a pesto, and use it on spaghetti. It makes an excellent chicken salad dressing. Other people use it as a dip for raw vegetables, or on crusty bread, or with split pita bread, toasted, cut into wedges. Try substituting 1½ cups canned white beans, drained and rinsed, for half of the bread. It's also wonderful as a spread on an open-faced sandwich on pumpernickel bread: smear it on generously, and top it with thick sliced tomatoes, or cucumbers with red onion, and lots of black pepper. A friend was given a cup of the stuff, took it home, added 8 oz. of Neufchatel cheese, and returned with a dip and a platter of sugar snap peas and mushroom halves – fantastic.

The idea of calm exists in a sitting cat. Jules Reynard

PINK AIOLI

2 slices bread, crusts removed, shredded or cut into 1" cubes

10 cloves garlic, minced

½ cup mayonnaise

½ cup sun-dried tomatoes in oil, rough chop

1 T. fresh lemon juice or wine vinegar

¼ tsp. red pepper flakes

½ cup olive oil

salt if necessary

Soak the bread in warm water for a few seconds, squeeze it out, and discard the water. Put the wet bread with everything except the olive oil into a processer and process briefly until blended. Add the oil in a thin stream until the mixture reaches a thick, dough-like consistency. Makes 2 cups.

Use this rich spread or dip with fresh raw vegetables, especially cauliflower, mushrooms, squashes, peppers, cukes, etc. Then try it with everything else you eat.

When a man's dog turns against him, it's time for a wife to pack her trunk and go home to mama. Mark Twain

ANNE'S SIMPLE GREEN SALSA MEXICANO

2 large cloves garlic, peeled

1 lb. fresh tomatillos, husked and washed

2 or 3 fresh serrano or jalapeno chili peppers

1 bunch fresh cilantro, chopped roughly

salt and pepper to taste

Dry-cook the garlic by heating it gently in a metal pan or pie tin without fat, watching and turning it as it slowly becomes soft and "yellow"; this takes about 10-15 minutes, and don't worry if some black spots appear – they just add to the flavor. Meanwhile, put the tomatillos and chilis into a medium-sized pan with an inch of water covering them and boil for 5-10 minutes or until they turn an olive color. Drain out ¾ of the water, and put the chilies and their remaining liquid into a processer or blender with all the rest of the ingredients. Process and adjust the seasoning, then put in a serving bowl and chill for an hour (it will thicken as it chills). Makes 2 cups.

If you have to peel lots of garlic cloves, soak the bulb in water in the refrigerator overnight; the cloves will come right out of their skins.

HEAT WAVE SALSA

2 very ripe mangos, peeled and cut into medium dice
4 scallions, chopped fine
2-4 jalapeño peppers, seeded and finely diced
¼ cup fresh cilantro, chopped fine
juice of 1 lime
salt to taste

Combine all the ingredients, taste for salt, and chill for at least an hour to let the flavors mingle. Try making it also with very ripe melon, peaches, or pineapple; or avocado (not too ripe) with a pinch of sugar added. It's good with everything, even chips! Makes 2 cups.

PEACHY SALSA

4 large peaches, skinned and cut into small cubes
1 T. fresh ginger, slivered or grated
the zest of 1 orange
¼ tsp. red pepper flakes
2 T. fresh cilantro, minced
2 T lime juice
1 T. brown sugar

Blend all the ingredients except the last two in a bowl. Shake the lime juice and brown sugar together in a small jar, pour them over the fruit, and let it marinate, covered, at room temperature for an hour. (Any tropical fruit will work in this salsa: mango, melon, pineapple, or papaya.) Makes about 2 cups.

Spray or oil utensil before measuring honey or molasses.

SUSAN'S STRAWBERRY STUFF

1 12-oz. pkg. frozen whole strawberries, thawed

¼ cup orange juice

1 T. lime juice

¼ cup orange-flavored liqueur

1 tsp. sugar

Blend all the ingredients in a blender or processer. Serve it on ice cream, sherbet, waffles, or yogurt, or just eat it with a spoon. Makes about 2 cups.

ELLEN'S RASPBERRY COULIS

1 12-oz. pkg. frozen raspberries, somewhat thawed

¼ cup sugar, or to taste

optional: 1 tsp. lemon juice or 1 T. orange-flavored liqueur

Puree in a blender or processer, strain it through a sieve, and it's done. Very handy kept in one of those plastic squeeze bottles you use for ketchup – you can make designs with it. For Valentine's Day, if a puddle of cream sauce surrounds dessert, for instance, drop dots of red all around the dish and then run a toothpick through them: they'll become hearts! Serves 4.

Even overweight cats instinctively know the cardinal rule: when fat, arrange yourself in slim poses. John Weitz

LIME SILK SAUCE - A MICROWAVE MUST

½ cup sugar
1 ½ T. water
¼ cup fresh lime juice
1/3 cup heavy cream
rind of 1 lime, grated

In a 2-cup glass vessel, place the sugar, the water, and 2 T. of the lime juice. Cover it very tightly (including the spout, and handle if present). Microwave on HIGH for 4-5 minutes, watching it like a hawk for the first signs of color change; when that occurs, remove the vessel from the oven, very carefully prick and peel off the wrap, and slowly stir in the cream. Cook uncovered for 30 seconds, remove, and stir in the rest of the lime juice and the rind. If pale makes you uneasy, add 1 drop of green food color. Incredible with chocolate anything; nifty with vanilla ice cream. You'll dream up a million uses. Makes 1 cup.

QUICK NECTARINE SAUCE

4 very fresh nectarines, peeled, pitted and cut up
1 tsp. ginger, fresh (or 2 tsp. crystallized), minced
4 T. honey (if fresh ginger is used)
4 T. lemon, lime or orange juice, or to taste

Combine everything in a blender or processer. Serve the sauce on sherbet, fresh fruit, yogurt, or in drinks like sangria.

The best way to avoid a fat cat is to get another cat. Anon

MEG'S CRACKLY SAUCE FOR ICE CREAM

1 cup brown sugar

2 T. molasses

¼ cup butter (4 T.)

1 ½ T. water

pinch of salt

1 T. vinegar

1/3 cup sliced almonds, toasted

Put all but the almonds in a saucepan and cook the mixture over high heat until it's almost hard crack (280 on a candy thermometer, or drip some into a glass of cold water to see if it is solid). Immediately stir in the almonds and pour the sauce over dishes of vanilla ice cream. Serves 6-8.

Definitely a candidate for The Institute of Short-Lived Phenomena, this choice sauce is a one-shot deal: it hardens as it hits the cold ice cream, and cannot be saved for an encore. Which is why we make it in small amounts. So if you have a dozen bowls of ice cream to cover, double the amount.

Dogs come when they are called; cats take a message and get back to you. Mary Bly

EIGHT-MINUTE KILLER CHOCOLATE SAUCE

2½ squares unsweetened chocolate, cut in pieces

½ cup cold water

¾ cup sugar

dash of salt

optional: 1-2 T. coffee or liqueur

Cook the chocolate and water together over direct medium heat for 4 minutes, stirring constantly. Don't worry if the chocolate turns oily. Add the sugar and the salt, still stirring, and cook for 4 minutes longer. Serve hot; when it cools and you are ready to put it away, you may want to add coffee or liqueur if it seems too thick. Stored in a covered container, it lasts indefinitely. Makes about 1 cup.

GLORIOUS MUD SAUCE

4 squares bittersweet (not unsweetened) chocolate

1 T. butter

6 T. heavy cream

2 T. Kahlúa (or brandy or rum)

Melt the chocolate with the butter and cream in a microwave oven or in a small bowl set over a pan of barely simmering water, whisking until it's smooth. Remove it from the heat and blend in the Kahlúa. Makes about 1 cup.

For a gotta-have-it-now chocolate covering/frosting, simply melt 3 ounces of unsweetened chocolate, chopped, with ½ cup of strong coffee (espresso, if you like), and stir in a box of powdered sugar. Use it at once – half the recipe is all you need for just drizzling.

DESSERTS
·&·
PASTRIES

10 Ideas for Gilding the Lily

1   Shower a casserole or salad with edible flowers or petals: roses, calendulas, nasturtiums, violets, marigolds, apple blossoms, lilacs, pansies, scented geraniums, johnny jump-ups, or daylilies.

2   Brownies: just before baking, sprinkle them with brickle bits or mini chocolate chips.

3   Brownies: reserve half of the batter; pour one half into the pan, and freeze it for 10 minutes. Spread it with raspberry jam, and add the rest of the batter. Wait 20 minutes and bake.

4   Desserts in chilled thin-stemmed glasses: before filling them, scatter powdered sugar everywhere – on the outside of the glass (turn it upside down) and on the base of the stem.

5   Desserts: crystallize rose petals or violets by painting them with lightly beaten eggwhites, laying them on a rack and sprinkling them with superfine sugar; then drying them in the refrigerator.

6   Baked beans, large can: add tomatoes, drained from a 20-oz. can; ½ bell pepper, diced; 1 large onion, diced and browned; ½ tsp. red pepper flakes; ¼ cup brown sugar; 2 T. molasses; salt and pepper. Mix everything and bake at 350 for an hour.

7   Baked beans again: do what a painter in Port Clyde does with his beans – cut a ½" slice off the top of a nice big onion and cut the sides off, too, making it into a cube. Rub a bit of butter on the top, place it in the center, (don't bury it). When the beans are done, it comes out looking quite fetching – a browned onion cube!

8   Fresh cantaloupe or honeydew: halve it horixontally, then peel and seed it; cut it into rings, and place a ring on each plate. In the center, put a few berries and a sprig of mint.

9   Melon: cut it into wedges and carefully separate the rind from the flesh, but keep them together. Cut each wedge into ¾" slices, and push every other one a bit to the left so that the finished product looks like saw teeth. Garnish with a tiny mint sprig.

10 Desserts: sauces around them can have designs of a contrasting color added by using a plastic squeeze bottle. Fill it with a paler cream or a darker puree and draw leaves and tendrils, squiggles, or zig-zags, etc.

your favorite piecrust

1 qt. in-season Maine strawberries, raspberries, or blueberries

2 cups lime curd with honey

powdered sugar for garnish

Bake and cool the crust in your favorite tart pan, prepare the fruit, and make the lime curd with honey:

4 egg yolks

1 cup sugar

¼ cup honey

3 or 4 bright green, healthy limes: ½ cup juice and 2 T. zest

5 oz. butter, cut in pieces

Beat the egg yolks until they're light, add the sugar, and continue beating until the mix is thick and pale. Beat in the honey. Put the juice, zest, and butter into the top of a double boiler over simmering water, and add the egg mixture. Whisk steadily, cooking the mixture in the double boiler until it becomes thick enough to coat a spoon and has a custard-like consistency, about 10 minutes. Do not overcook. Take the curd off the stove and, if you wish, strain it, pushing it through a sieve with a wooden spoon, and discarding the zest. (Some people prefer leaving the zest in.) Put the curd into a covered container and refrigerate it (where it will last for months) until needed. To assemble the dessert, spread the lime curd over the pastry crust, cover it with a layer of fruit, and chill. Just before serving, sprinkle powdered sugar over the top. Vanilla ice cream, anyone? Serves 8-10 .

We made our lime zest by removing very thin strips with a vegetable peeler and putting them into one of those tiny food processors – works like a charm in no time at all, and eliminates grated knuckles as an ingredient.

JADE'S RASPBERRY BLUEBERRY PIE

1 pint fresh raspberries, or 12-oz. pkg. frozen, thawed

1 quart fresh Maine wild blueberries, or other blueberries

½ cup sugar

3 T. cornstarch

a pinch of salt

1 baked pie crust, cooled

Make a puree by pressing the raspberries through a sieve with a wooden pestle or spoon; you should have 1 cup. In a small saucepan, blend it with one cup of the blueberries, the sugar, cornstarch, and salt, and stir it over low heat until it's just boiling: it should be thick and transparent. Add 2 cups more of the blueberries and cook until it bubbles again. Cool. These steps can be taken well before the pie is served. To assemble it, simply pour the filling into the prepared pie crust and spread the last cup of fresh blueberries over the top. Serve vanilla ice cream on the side, if you like. (Some people like to save 2 cups of berries for the top; it's up to you – in which case, add just 1 cup more for the second bubbling.) Serves 6-8.

For a dashing dessert, paint the inside layer of several layers of pleated foil or paper baking cups with ¼" of melted chocolate or melted chocolate mixed with ground toasted nuts. Chill them in muffin tins, then gently peel off the paper and fill them with ice cream or sherbet.

GLAZED SUMMER STRAWBERRY PIE

¾ cup graham cracker crumbs

1 cup walnut or pecan crumbs, toasted

3 T. sugar

4 T. butter, melted

optional: 1 T. orange rind

5 cups fresh strawberries, washed and hulled

3 T. cornstarch

¾ cups orange juice

½-¾ cup sugar

1 tsp. lemon juice

1 T. orange-flavored liqueur

fresh mint leaves for garnish

Make the crust: Blend the first 3 ingredients (and orange rind if desired) in a bowl, stir in the melted butter, and pat the mixture onto the bottom and sides of a 10" pie pan. Chill. Reserve 3 cups of the nicest berries and place them on a towel to dry. Crush the rest of the berries and put them in a pan. Whisk the cornstarch with the orange juice and mix it in with the berries. Add the sugar, tasting for sweetness, and cook, stirring, over medium-low heat until the glaze is clear and thick, about 10 minutes. Chill it slightly before adding the lemon juice and liqueur. Arrange the whole berries with their tips up in the pie shell and spoon the glaze over them. Cool, garnish, and serve. Serves 6-8.

Keep a vanilla bean in a jar of sugar for baking and making desserts. Replace the sugar every time you use it.

MOUSE MILKER'S GRAPE PIE

4 cups (2 lb.) Concord grapes, skins separated from pulp

¾ cups sugar

optional: 1 T. orange rind

2 T. lemon juice

1 T. tapioca or 2 tsp. cornstarch

1 T. butter

pie crust for a double crust 9" pie

(You'll be surprised at how quick and easy it is to skin Concord grapes, especially for an obsessive, task-oriented person: simply squeeze the grape. Out pops the pulp – you're holding the skin.) Put the grape skins in one saucepan, and the pulp in another. Cook them both: the skins until tender, the pulp until soft. Using a colander or sieve, strain the pulp from the seeds and combine it with the skins. Add the sugar, orange rind, lemon juice, and tapioca and cook a little longer to dissolve the sugar. Preheat the oven to 450; line a pie pan with the pastry, fill it with the grape mixture, dot with butter, and top it with a lattice crust. Bake it for 10 minutes, lower the heat to 325, and bake for another 20 minutes. This is a unique and utterly delicious pie which can be served alone. O.K., maybe a wee bit of ice cream on the side. Serves 6-8.

'Tis a brave mouse who makes her nest in a cat's ear.

BELFAST BLUEBERRY CRISP

4 T. butter, sliced in ½" pieces

4 T. brown sugar, packed

½ cup flour

½ cup slivered almonds, toasted

1 quart Maine blueberries

1 lemon: zest and juice

2 T. instant tapioca or flour

4 T. sugar

pinch of ground cinnamon

optional: 1 cup ricotta cheese mixed with 2 T. honey or sugar

Preheat the oven to 400. Put the first 4 ingredients into a processer, pulsing briefly to mix, or blend them in a bowl as you would a piecrust. It can be lumpy – this is the topping. In a separate bowl, mix the berries with ½ of the lemon juice, ½ of the zest, the flour, the sugar, and the cinnamon. Put them into a 1-quart baking dish and "thumb" the topping over them, distributing it as evenly as you can. Bake the crisp for 20-25 minutes and serve it with ice cream or sweetened ricotta: blend the ricotta mix with the rest of the lemon juice and rind. Serves 4-6.

If you must stop a dogfight – and it takes two people – try a loud distraction other than shouting (which may excite them further) and then each person pull a dog by the hind legs, separating them. However, do not attempt this unless one of the dogs is in danger – it is safer to let the dogs settle things themselves.

ALLIGATOR PEAR CREAM

2 large avocados, peeled and cut into large pieces
1/3 cup sugar
¼ cup half-and-half cream
¼ cup lime juice and zest of 1 lime
2 T. tequila
dash of salt

Blend or process all the ingredients, pulsing on and off and scraping down the sides with a rubber spatula as you go, until the dessert is completely smooth. Spoon it into small cups, chill for a few hours, covered, garnish, and serve. Makes 2 cups; serves 6.

If you have a bartender's zester, try collecting thin strips from a lime and cooking them in a pan with 1 T. sugar and 1 T. water until they're thick and candied, about 4 or 5 minutes. Put them on wax paper until serving time, and top the desserts with a dollop of sour cream and the candied lime.

Since each of us is blessed with only one life, why not live it with a cat. Robert Stearns

GRANDMA OLIVE'S PAINLESS POTS DE CREME

1 6-oz. pkg. chocolate bits

1 egg

2 T. flavoring: cointreau, kahlua, vanilla

¾ cup scalded milk, minus 2 T.

Put everything into a blender except the hot milk, which you will add while the machine is running. When it is smooth, pour the mixture into thin glass cups. Chill them and garnish with sour cream and orange peel, shaved chocolate, crystallized or fresh violets, etc. Serves 6.

God forbid that I should go to any heaven in which there are no horses. Robert Cunningham-Graham, in a letter to Theodore Roosevelt

CHOCOLATE PÂTÉ

15 oz. bittersweet chocolate

1 cup heavy cream

4 T. sweet butter, cut up

4 egg yolks

1 cup powdered sugar, sifted

½ cup dark rum

fresh raspberries, chocolate shavings, or crystallized violets for
  garnish

In a double boiler, or a bowl set over hot water, or a microwave oven on HIGH for 2 minutes, melt the chocolate, cream, and butter, stirring if necessary. Whisk in the egg yolks, one at a time, and then gradually whisk in the sugar and the rum. Line the bottom and sides of a small (1 quart) loaf pan with plastic wrap, leaving plenty of overhang. Pour in the mixture, and let it cool to room temperature. Then wrap it and refrigerate it overnight. Invert the loaf onto a serving platter and keep it chilled until you're ready to serve. Decorate it and cut it with a cold knife or wire cheese cutter into ½" slices. Ellen's Raspberry Coulis? Sour cream, anyone? Serves 8-10.

Actually, Lime Silk Sauce would not go amiss here – perhaps with a sprinkling of gently toasted pistachios alongside – if the boss is coming to dinner.

A dog is prose, a cat is a poem. Jean Burden

THAT LEGENDARY COFFEE-TOFFEE PIE

1 cup piecrust mix from a package

¼ cup brown sugar, packed firmly

¾ cup walnuts, toasted and finely chopped

1 square unsweetened chocolate, grated

1 tsp. vanilla

½ cup (1 stick) sweet butter

¾ cup superfine granulated sugar

1 square unsweetened chocolate, melted

2 tsp. instant espresso coffee powder

2 eggs

pinch of salt

2 cups heavy cream

2 T. instant espresso coffee powder

½ cup powdered sugar

chocolate curls for garnish

Begin this pie the day before you need it, or start it early in the day. Preheat the oven to 375, and make the pastry shell: combine the first 5 ingredients, blend them well, and press firmly against the sides and bottom of a 9" well-greased pie plate. Bake for 15 minutes and cool on a wire rack. Make the filling: in a small bowl with an electric beater, cream the butter, add the sugar, and beat until fluffy. Blend in the next 2 ingredients, and add 1 egg; beat 3 minutes. Add the other egg and the pinch of salt and beat 3 minutes more. Pour it into the baked shell and refrigerate, covered, overnight. At the same time, combine the cream with the coffee powder and sugar in a covered container and refrigerate it. A few hours before you need the pie, make the topping: beat the cream until stiff. Decorate the pie with the cream, using a pastry bag and fluted decorating tip, or smooth it over the top with a spatula, garnishing with chocolate curls or those chocolate-covered espresso beans. Refrigerate the pie for 2 hours. Serves 8.

This is one pie definitely worth the effort. It's a pie for your father's 70th birthday, or for your 40th high school reunion pajama party.

LISSA'S WHITE CHOCOLATE VELVET CHEESECAKE

¾ cup graham cracker crumbs

2 T. sugar

¼ cup (½ stick) butter, melted

24 oz. light cream cheese

2 large eggs

8 oz. good quality white chocolate, melted

2 T. half-and-half cream

¾ cup light sour cream

Preheat the oven to 350. Make the crust by combining the first 3 ingredients, and pressing them onto the bottom of an 8" springform pan. For the filling, blend the next 3 ingredients in a machine, add the creams, and combine thoroughly. Pour it into the crust and bake for 45 minutes without peeking. The cake will be slightly soft in the center, but will firm as it cools. After 45 minutes, turn off the oven and prop open the door a crack with a potholder or a knife, to allow the cake to cool for an hour. Then refrigerate it to chill. Serve it with strawberry or raspberry sauce and white chocolate shavings; perhaps a mint leaf or two. (An alternate crust might be an Oreo one: 24 cream-filled cookies crushed, instead of the graham crackers. Omit sugar, same butter.) Serves 8-10.

If you start your kitten early traveling often in the car for short trips to the grocery store or to visit grandparents, and reward it when it arrives home, it will not behave badly in the car, even when going to the veterinarian.

SIMPLE, SUMPTUOUS FOUR-CHOCOLATE CHEESECAKE

1 ½ cups chocolate wafer crumbs (27-30, or 6 oz.)

1/3 cup unsweetened cocoa

½ cup powdered sugar

1/3 cup butter, melted

1 ½ cups semi-sweet chocolate bits (9 oz.)

3 oz. unsweetened chocolate

3 8-oz. pkgs. cream cheese, regular or Neufchatel

4 eggs

1 can (14 oz.) sweetened condensed milk

2 tsp. vanilla

¼ cup coffee-flavored liqueur

1 T. instant espresso coffee powder

Combine the first 4 ingredients in a bowl or processer and press the mixture onto the bottom of a 10" springform pan. Reserve. Preheat the oven to 300. In a small bowl, melt the chocolate over hot water and reserve. In a processer, or in a large bowl, beat the cream cheese until it's fluffy and slowly add the rest of the ingredients, including the chocolate, beating until smooth. Pour the batter into the prepared pan and bake it for 65 minutes or until the center is set. Cool the cake and then chill it . When you're ready to serve it, run a sharp knife around the edge before turning it out. Garnish like mad – you know what to do! Serves 14-16.

We found a fern leaf in the back yard and laid it on top of the cooled cake, shook cocoa in a sieve over it, carefully removed the leaf, and left a nifty stencilled design.

VINNIE'S VANISHING PEARS

6 medium pears, not too ripe, peeled, halved, and cored

4 T. sugar

1/3 stick sweet butter

1 cup heavy cream

Preheat the oven to 425. Place the pear halves flat side down, in a single layer in one or two baking dishes. Sprinkle the sugar over them, dot with butter, and bake them for 35 minutes, or until the sugar has caramelized and the pears are tender. Pour the cream over the pears and return them to the oven. Bake 15 minutes more, basting every few minutes with the cream, which should reduce and thicken and turn golden. If the sauce seems to separate, add 1-2 tablespoons of hot water. Remove the pears from the oven, allow them to cool a little, and serve them directly from the baking dish – within ten minutes of leaving the oven. Serves 6

Cats, like men, are flatterers. W. S. Landor

GARDEN STRAWBERRIES CUTTING EDGE

just-picked strawberries, washed and hulled

pink or black peppercorns, cracked

very good balsamic vinegar

optional: sour cream

Try serving the freshest strawberries you can find, whole or sliced, in bowls topped with either a sprinkle of cracked pink peppercorns, or else with black peppercorns and a splash of balsamic vinegar. Sour cream anywhere you like. Serves any number.

BALSAMIC STRAWBERRY SORBET

1/3 cup sugar

1/3 cup orange juice or water

1 T. cracked black pepper

1 pint fresh strawberries, washed and stemmed

1 T. balsamic vinegar

The odd and delicious combination above – very Italian – also makes an equally snazzy sorbet: bring to a boil the first 3 ingredients, and cool it while you puree a pint of fresh strawberries, and add to it 1 T. balsamic vinegar. Combine all of the ingredients, chill them, and freeze them in an ice cream maker, according to the manufacturer's directions. Makes 1 pint.

You don't train cats, they train you. Ivy Dodd

CHILLY SORBET

1 cup boiling water

1 hot chili pepper, seeded and minced

zest of 1 lime

2 cups limeade concentrate

Pour the water over the chili and lime, and allow to cool for 20 minutes. Stir in the concentrate, chill the mixture, and freeze it in an ice cream maker, following the manufacturer's directions. Makes about 3 cups.

WATERMELON SORBET

1/3 cup sugar

1 T. fresh lime or lemon juice

1 T. limeade or lemonade concentrate

3 pints watermelon, cut up, seeds removed

In a tiny saucepan, over low heat, combine the first 3 ingredients, stirring until they're dissolved. Let them cool while you puree the watermelon (you'll need about 3 ½ cups), and then combine it with the syrup. Chill it and freeze it in an ice cream maker, following the manufacturer's directions. Makes about a quart.

DOG'S BREATH SORBET

1 ¼ cups unsweetened cocoa

½ cup sugar

2 cups strong hot coffee

¼ cup sweet vermouth, sherry, or brandy

Combine the cocoa with the sugar in a bowl, and whisk in the coffee to dissolve and blend the mix. Add the vermouth, chill it, and freeze it in an ice cream maker, following the manufacturer's directions. Makes about 3 cups.

PEPPERMINT PATTY ICE CREAM

1 pint vanilla ice cream

6 medium-sized peppermint patties

Allow the ice cream to soften. Cut the mints into small pieces, add them to the ice cream, and mix thoroughly. Put into a covered container. Freeze. Peppermint Patty lives!! Serves 2-3.

Remember ice cream sandwiches? You can make them yourself – just get some of those thin chocolate wafers, the nice expensive kind, and put a couple of tablespoons of ice cream between two of them. (You can use any favorite cookie for this, of course.) Freeze them on a baking sheet, covered, until they are hard, and then pop each one into a sandwich bag for storage in the freezer.

GINGER ICE CREAM IN A TWINKLING

1 quart vanilla ice cream

½ cup crystallized (candied) ginger, chopped

2 T. ginger marmalade or conserve

1 tsp. fresh ginger root, minced

optional: 1 envelope powdered ginger tea or ginger drink
(Chinese markets)

Allow the ice cream to soften, mix in all the ingredients, and freeze it. Rather special with chocolate sauce. Might be good in an ice cream sandwich, too (see above). Serves 4.

If a horse won't take the bit, try rubbing it with molasses.

ESME'S AMBROSIAL COMPOTE

    1 16-oz. can black cherries plus juice
    1 16-oz. can pear halves plus juice
    1 navel orange, rough chopped, skin included
    ½ lb. dried apricots
    the zest of 1 lemon
    1 stick cinnamon
    ½ cup brown sugar

Preheat the oven to 250. Put everything into a casserole; the juice should just cover the fruit. Bake it uncovered for 1 hour; turn the oven up to 300, give the mixture a stir, and continue baking for 1 hour more. Serve the compote at room temperature with your choice of cream. Serves 6-8

If you give a puppy an old slipper or sneaker to chew, he will probably think that all shoes are fair game. Give it toys of hard rubber with no loose parts that might break off and be swallowed.

MORRIE'S DOUBLE CHOCOLATE WALNUT BISCOTTI

2 cups all-purpose flour

½ cup unsweetened cocoa

1 tsp. baking soda

1 tsp. salt

7 T. unsalted butter, softened

1 cup granulated sugar

2 large eggs

2 tsp. orange extract

zest of one orange

1 cup walnuts, toasted

¾ cup semisweet chocolate bits

2 T. powdered sugar

Preheat the oven to 350 and butter and flour (or cocoa) a large baking sheet. In a bowl, whisk together the four dry ingredients. In another bowl with an electric mixer, beat together the softened butter and the sugar until light and fluffy. Add the eggs, extract, and zest and beat until well blended. Stir in the flour mixture to form a stiff dough. Stir in the walnuts and chocolate bits. Drop the dough by large spoonfuls into two long columns on the baking sheet, using floured hands and a spatula to form it into two slightly flattened logs, each 12 inches long and 2 inches wide. Dust them with powdered sugar and bake for 35 minutes or until slightly firm to the touch. Cool them for 5 minutes on the baking sheet. On a cutting board, cut the biscotti diagonally into ¾" slices and arrange them, cut sides down, on the sheet; bake until crisp, about 10 more minutes. Cool them on a rack and store them in air-tight containers where they will keep for a week. If frozen, they will last a month. Makes about 30.

The biggest dog has been a pup. Joaquin Miller

MYRNA'S CHOCOLATE COCONUT MACAROONS

3 egg whites

½ cup sugar

1 tsp. vanilla

3 oz. bittersweet chocolate, melted

3 oz. (½ cup) chocolate bits, melted

8 oz. shredded coconut

Preheat oven to 350. Slowly beat the egg whites until they're light and, still beating, add the sugar a little at a time. Fold in the vanilla, then the chocolate and coconut and drop the batter by rounded tablespoons, ½" apart, onto greased cookie sheets. Bake for 15 minutes and remove from the sheets at once to cool on wire racks. (Hint: coconut usually comes in 7-oz. packages; be sure to use 8 ounces or the cookies will come out flat.) Makes about 2 dozen.

You can vary the recipe by substituting ½ cup finely chopped maraschino cherries for the chocolate – press them dry in a sieve with a wooden spoon and then squeeze in paper towels. Decorate each one with a quarter of a cherry pressed down into the top.

Teach children to stay away from a strange dog unless the owner is present.

1/3 cup butter, melted

2 cups oatmeal

½ cup brown sugar

¼ cup dark corn syrup

½ tsp. salt, or to taste

1½ tsp. vanilla

1 cup chocolate bits

1 or 2 squares bittersweet chocolate, chopped

½ cup nuts, toasted and chopped

Preheat the oven to 450. Pour the melted butter over the oatmeal in a bowl and mix them well. Add everything except the chocolate and nuts and pack the mixture firmly into a greased 7x11 non-stick pan. Bake it for 12 minutes and remove it from the oven; it should be golden and bubbling. Combine the chocolate in a bowl and sprinkle it on top, smoothing it after a few minutes with a rubber spatula. Sprinkle it with the nuts, pressing them gently into the top. Cool, cut, and serve during the game. Makes about 16 pieces.

Histories are more full of examples of fidelity of dogs than of friends. Alexander Pope

POST OFFICE BROWNIES

4 squares unsweetened chocolate

¾ cup (1 ½ sticks) butter

2 cups sugar

3 eggs, lightly beaten

1 T. instant espresso coffee powder

¼ tsp. salt

1 ½ tsp. vanilla

1 cup flour

1 ½ cups walnuts, toasted and rough chopped

Preheat the oven to 350. Prepare a 9x13 pan by buttering or spraying it and then coating it with cocoa. Melt the chocolate and the butter together in a medium-large saucepan (which will serve as your mixing bowl) over hot water. Remove it from the heat, add the sugar, and whisk in the eggs, blending them well. Mix in the coffee powder, salt, vanilla, and flour, and finally the nuts. Pour the batter into the pan, starting at the corners and finishing in the center. Bake the brownies for 25-30 minutes or until a toothpick comes out slightly crumby. If in doubt, take them out sooner rather than later. Allow them to cool thoroughly in the pan on a rack before cutting. Makes 2 dozen.

These brownies are made several times a year for the crew at a Boston Post Office by a grateful patron – always accompanied by a half-gallon of milk, a bunch of plastic cups, and some paper napkins.

A good toy for a puppy is a vacuum cleaner belt – it's perfect for tug-of-war.

BREAKFAST & BRUNCH

10 uses for Fresh Maine Blueberries

1   Drop onto pancakes while they are cooking on a griddle.

2   Fold into any yellow cake batter with a little cinnamon, or knead gently into scone or biscuit dough, topping with sugar.

3   Toss into a green salad with lime vinaigrette.

4   Make blueberry buttermilk for two: press ½ cup berries through a sieve and add it, with ½ tsp. orange or lemon rind and 1 tsp. of its juice, and 2 T. honey to 2 cups buttermilk. If it's breakfast, add a beaten egg.

5   Make blueberry ice cream cones: fill a cone almost to the top with berries and top it with a scoop of ice cream or sherbet. It will melt down into the berries.

6   Make instant sauce: simmer 1 cup of blueberries, 2-4 T. sugar, ½ cup orange juice, 1 tsp. orange rind, 1 T. cornstarch and ½ tsp. cinnamon until thick. Spoon over French toast or use as a dessert sauce.

7   Make blueberry vinegar: 1 pint berries, 1½ cups clear vinegar, and 3 T. sugar simmered for 5 minutes and refrigerated for 2 weeks to develop flavor; then strained and stored in the refrigerator. Use it in a salad, or combine it with honey for a fruit salad, or use it to rinse out the skillet when sautéing chicken or pork.

8   Dry them so you can make blueberry-chip cookies: spread them on a baking sheet and put them in a 200 oven for 6-8 hours or overnight.

9   Blueberry muffins, of course! (You've already thought of pie.)

10 Lie outside in a hammock with your book, and pop them into your mouth, one at a time.

SUMMER OF '86 BLUEBERRY MUFFIN BAKE-OFF WINNER

1½ cups flour

3 tsp. baking powder

½ cup sugar

½ cup milk

1 egg, beaten

¼ cup melted butter

1 cup blueberries

Preheat the oven to 375. Combine the dry ingredients in a bowl and sift three times. (Use a sieve if you have no sifter.) Reserve 2 T. of this for dredging the berries. Combine the milk and egg and add them to the dry ingredients. Add the melted butter, slightly cooled. Dredge the berries and fold them in carefully; the trick is to move the batter as little as possible. Spoon the mix into well-greased muffin tins, filling them 2/3 full, sprinkle the tops with a little sugar, and bake for 20-25 minutes. Makes a dozen .

You can make these your own trademark muffins by varying them a bit: for instance, adding grated orange or lemon rind, or vanilla extract, or a pinch of cinnamon. Experiment for the next bake-off.

A little drowsing cat is a picture of perfect beatitude. Champfleury

NANCIE'S MELT-IN-YOUR-MOUTH SCONES WITH GINGER

2 cups flour
1½ tsp. baking powder
¼ tsp. baking soda
1 stick butter, cut into pieces
½ cup cream
½ cup crystallized (candied) ginger, chopped

Preheat the oven to 375. Combine the first three ingredients very quickly in a processer, add the butter, and pulse until the mixture resembles crumbs. Or mix them in a bowl, cutting the butter in as you do for pie crust. Rapidly add the cream and the ginger (saving 2 T. for sprinkling on top), and turn the dough out onto a floured board. Knead it briefly (about 10 times), gather it into a round shape, and place on a greased cookie sheet. Flatten it out and cut it into eight wedges like a pie. Sprinkle the top with ginger and a little sugar, and bake it for 10-15 minutes. Makes 8 scones.

These fabulous scones can be made with anything: fresh berries, dried cranberries, or raisins soaked in brandy. They can also be made smaller by forming them into two rounds, cut into eight pieces each. Or make them into shortcakes for dessert, accompanied by ginger ice cream, chocolate sauce, toasted nuts, and whipped topping.

A litter of kittens or puppies has one mother, but may have several fathers.

WARREN'S 10-MINUTE TOASTER OVEN BISCUITS IN A PROCESSER

1 cup self-rising flour

1 T. powdered buttermilk

½ tsp. salt

2 T. cold butter, sliced into small pieces

1/3 cup cold milk or water

optional: 2 T. Gruyère or sharp cheddar cheese, grated or chopped

Preheat the toaster oven to 450. Place all the ingredients except the milk into the container of a processer and pulse until it achieves the consistency of corn meal. Put this mixture into a bowl and stir in enough milk to make a moist dough. Oil a small sheet of aluminum foil, drop spoonfuls of the batter onto it (touching each other or separate, it doesn't matter), and bake them for 10 minutes. Makes 6.

You can add anything to these: chopped bacon, herbs, olives, bits of meat, etc., and top them, too, with the chopped cheese, grated Parmesan, coarse salt, etc. Or make them sweet by substituting sugar for the salt and adding nuts or raisins soaked in warm brandy. Search the refrigerator for scraps and have fun.

If a cat does something, we call it instinct; if we do the same thing for the same reason, we call it intelligence. Will Cuppy

BARBARA MANN'S OCEAN HOUSE CODFISH CAKES

3 cups haddock or hake, poached and flaked

3 cups potatoes, cooked firm, then grated

3 eggs, beaten

1 medium onion, minced

stock from the fish (or ½ cup clam broth)

salt and white pepper to taste

3 T. flour

oil or butter for grill

Poach the fish ahead of time and refrigerate, saving its liquid. Chill the boiled (drained) potatoes as well, for easier grating. Reduce the fish stock to ½ cup (or use clam broth). Combine the fish and the potatoes in a large bowl and add the eggs, onion, stock, and salt and pepper. Sprinkle with the flour and blend. Shape the mixture into cakes and cook on both sides on a heated, oiled grill or frying pan – about 4 minutes on each side. Serves 8-10.

Leftover lobster wouldn't go amiss here – or crabmeat, either, if it's all you have in the house. How about chives instead of onion? Or parsley? Instead of tartar sauce, ketchup, or hot sauce, try Frances's Sauce (under Cushing Crab Cakes).

Dogs laugh, but they laugh with their tails. Max Eastman

GOUGÈRE - FOR BRUNCH OR COCKTAILS

1 cup milk

4 T. butter

1 tsp. salt

pinch of ground black pepper

1 cup flour

4 large eggs

1 cup Gruyère or Swiss cheese, cut into tiny cubes or grated

milk for brushing on top

Preheat the oven to 375. Put the first four ingredients into a medium-sized saucepan, bring to a boil, and immediately remove it from the heat. Add the flour all at once and, stirring madly with a wooden spoon, beat it until the mixture forms a ball and leaves the sides of the pan. Add the eggs, one at a time, beating with the wooden spoon until each one is thoroughly incorporated before adding the next one. When the dough is shiny and smooth, mix in ¾ cup of the cheese. Butter a baking sheet and either form a wreath on the sheet, by placing large oval spoonfuls in the proper shape and then adding smaller ones on top, or – for cocktails – simply place spoonfuls of batter onto the cookie sheet at least an inch apart. Sprinkle the remaining cheese on top, brush with milk, and bake for 35-45 minutes, until puffed and browned (for small puffs, bake 15-20 minutes). Serves 4 to 8.

The country is going to the dogs. Bernard Shaw

SUNDAY BREAKFAST POUF FOR JORDAN

½ cup flour
½ cup milk
2 eggs, beaten
pinch of nutmeg
3 T. butter
2 T. powdered sugar
juice of half a lemon

Preheat the oven to 425. Put a large cast-iron skillet in to heat. Blend the first 4 ingredients in a bowl. Combine them gently; leave the batter a bit lumpy. A minute or two before you bake it, put the butter in the skillet to melt. Pour in the batter and bake it for 15-20 minutes, until it's golden brown and puffy. It will soon curl over and flop, but don't panic; that's normal. Sprinkle it with the sugar, return it briefly to the oven, and just before you serve it, sprinkle with the lemon juice. If you double the recipe, and have a huge cast-iron skillet, bake it for 20-25 minutes, and use 5 T. butter. Otherwise do it in two skillets, doubling as usual. Serves 2-4.

If you're feeling adventurous, leave out the nutmeg and instead, add 1 T. fresh lavender blossoms, chopped, to the batter. Garnish with stems of lavender and sprinkle with lavender sugar: process 1 part blossoms and 2 parts sugar together. (For permanent sugar, put 10-12 stems into a jar with 2 cups of sugar; it will be ready in 10-14 days. Use it for sprinkling on fruit, muffins, pies, etc., and in cookie dough, and replace sugar when used.)   Another way to flavor the pouf is with ¼ tsp. coarsely ground black peppercorns and ½ tsp. lemon or lime zest instead of the nutmeg. Use the juice, but no powdered sugar. This version is nice at brunch, but even better with drinks at sunset.

Cats are always elegant. John Weitz

CHOLESTEROL-FREE BREAKFAST CORN PUFF

1 carton egg substitute (1 cup; 4 eggs), room temperature

½ tsp. baking powder

1 T. cake flour

3 T. low-fat plain yogurt

1 tsp. jalapeño pepper, minced

¼ tsp. cracked black pepper

½ cup corn: fresh, frozen, or canned

1 T. fresh cilantro, minced

1 T. olive oil

2 T. scallions, minced

¼ cup pepper jack cheese, shredded

Beat the "eggs" with an electric beater until they are doubled in volume and very thick. Whisk the baking powder, flour, and yogurt together in a small bowl, add it to the eggs, and beat for 10 seconds. Fold in the next 4 ingredients and reserve. Preheat the broiler. Heat a 10" cast-iron skillet, add the olive oil, and sauté the scallions for a few minutes. Pour in the egg mix, sprinkle it with the cheese, and pop the whole thing under the broiler for about 7 minutes, or until it is still damp but brown and puffy. Serve it at once. Serves 3.

Prevent pets from chewing on electrical cords by rubbing the cords with a bar of strong laundry soap — try the hardware store.

FRENCH TOAST OOH LA LA

2 eggs, beaten

2/3 cup milk

1 loaf unsliced bread, any kind

fillings such as sliced fresh fruit in season, artichoke hearts,
mushrooms, ham and honey mustard, crabmeat or lobster
salad, fresh berries, etc.

Mix the egg and the milk, adding ½ tsp. vanilla and 1 tsp. sugar if
the filling is a sweet one, and salt and pepper if not. Cut
double-thick slices of bread, slit each one through the middle, but
not quite all the way across, and tuck the filling inside. Close the
slice, dip it into the egg mix, and cook it in the usual way.
Serves 4-6.

Variations: substitute ½ cup condensed tomato soup for the milk
and use cheese bread. Try cinnamon toast, tomato bread, or
brioche loaf. Serve the toast with a pesto thinned with yogurt or
sour cream, a fruit sauce, syrup, sherbet – whatever you like.

Le chat s'en va, les souris dansent. (When the cat's away . . .)

ENGLISH MUFFIN PUDDING FOR DILLON

2 eggs

salt, pepper, and adobe spice to taste

2 cups warm milk

3 English muffins, stale or fresh, split

1 small can corn

2 cups pepper jack or other sharp cheese, shredded

optional: red bell pepper and/or jalapeño, chopped

Preheat the oven to 350. Whisk the eggs and spices into the milk. Oil an ovenproof baking dish and place the muffin halves, cut side up, in overlapping rows on the bottom. Pour on the milk mixture, then sprinkle on the corn and the cheese and bake for 30-45 minutes, until they're golden. Let them cool, and serve with salsa or hot pepper jelly. Serves 4.

Make instant gloves for the safe handling of hot peppers — simply rub vegetable oil on your hands.

MARGARET'S BAD-FOR-YOU BRUNCH

2 cups corn flakes, crushed

½ cup butter, melted

2 lb. frozen hash-brown potatoes

½ cup onions, chopped

1 can cream-of-chicken soup

1 lb. cheddar cheese, shredded

1 pint sour cream

¼ tsp. pepper

1 tsp. salt

Preheat the oven to 350. Combine ¼ cup of the melted butter with the corn flakes and reserve it for the topping. Mix all the other ingredients and put into a large (3-4 quart) shallow baking dish. Add the topping and bake it for 1 hour, or until the top is golden. This dish can be prepared the night before and refrigerated, if you like. Bake it in the morning. Serves 4-6.

Newfoundland dogs are good to save children from drowning, but you must have a pond of water handy and a child, or else there will be no profit in boarding a Newfoundland. Josh Billings

CHICK PEA FLOUR CHIVE PANCAKE

1 cup chick pea flour (health food store or food co-op)

1 cup warm water

¼ tsp. hot red pepper flakes, or to taste

¼ tsp. salt, or to taste

¼ cup fresh chives, chopped

oil for frying

Combine the ingredients in a small bowl. Heat 1 T. of the oil in a frying pan until very hot, and pour in one large pancake, turning it when the edges are brown. Keep it hot in the oven while you finish the batter. Serve the pancakes with a dipping sauce of 4 T. soy sauce, 4 T. balsamic vinegar, ½ tsp. minced garlic, ½ tsp. ginger, and hot pepper sauce to taste. Makes 4 pancakes.

This is the tenderest and most delectable dish – outrageously easy to make. Chick pea flour, if you can get it, has a marvelous, nutty flavor. It also makes a fantastic polenta, in half the time of the usual one, in a two-to-one proportion of cold broth to flour. There's another chick pea pancake that is famous in the south of France, and it is made by mixing 7/8 cup chick pea flour, 1 cup water, 3 T. olive oil, and ¼ tsp. salt, and allowing it to stand for an hour. Half of it is poured into a large cast-iron pan which has been heated in a 500 degree oven and spread with olive oil. It is put under the broiler, as close to the flame as possible, and, after a few minutes more oil is scattered on it, and it is cooked for another 5 minutes, becoming brown and crisp around the edges. It is served on a warm plate, salted and peppered and cut into wedges. Repeat for the other half of the batter. You can buy these on the streets all over Nice – nice, no?

The great pleasure of a dog is that you may make a fool of yourself with him and not only will he not scold you, but he will make a fool of himself too. Samuel Butler

BIG BOARD BRUNCH FOR A PARTY

¼ cup butter, melted

½ loaf good egg bread, or your choice, sliced

8 - 10 eggs

1/3 cup cream

1/3 cup fresh chives, chopped

salt and pepper to taste

½ lb. smoked salmon, flaked or cut into 2" pieces

2-4 oz. salmon roe or red whitefish caviar

small bunch of chives, rough chopped, for garnish

Preheat the broiler. Butter a large cookie sheet, arrange the bread slices on it to fit tightly together, and brush the bread with more butter. Put it briefly under the broiler until it is lightly toasted. Meanwhile, whisk the eggs with the cream, chives, and salt and pepper and scramble them until firm but not quite done. Spread the eggs on the bread, pop the pan into the oven (300) for 5 minutes or so, just until set. Let it cool for a minute or two, slip it onto a heated platter, sprinkle with the salmon, and garnish with the caviar and chives. Serves 8.

Charley likes to get up early, and he likes me to get up early too. And why shouldn't he? Right after his breakfast he goes back to sleep.
John Steinbeck

CREATURE COMFORTS

10 Things to Roll Up in a Large Flour Tortilla or Split Pita Bread

1   Of course, any pesto plus leftovers and shredded lettuce for a sandwich.

2   Cream cheese and olives plus jalapeños or drained salsa, rolled up, chilled, and cut into slices for appetizers.

3   Combine 3 oz. cream cheese, ¼ cup minced chives and one small hard-boiled egg. Spread, roll, wrap in plastic and chill. Slice, and top with ½ tsp. caviar for appetizers.

4   Port Clyde Crabmeat Spread or Wicked Good Artichoke Spread, rolled up, heated, chilled and sliced; served as an appetizer.

5   Thinly applied anchovy paste, shredded mozzarella or pepper jack cheese, thin sliced tomatoes, chopped Greek olives and slivered garlic, rolled and heated until the cheese melts.

6   For the kids, how about P.B. and J.?

7   Make a casserole by filling 4-6 with crabmeat or lots of a grilled veg, packing them into a baking dish, and spooning a creamy, cheesy, or thinned-out pesto sauce around them.

8   Sliced ham, mustard and brie, melted. Roast beef with horse-radish mayo, capers, and shredded lettuce, warm or cold.

9   Another casserole: 3 or 4 asparagus spears rolled in a ricotta-spread flour tortilla, covered with a slice of mozzarella and a cream sauce with Parmesan sprinkled on top – several of these in a baking dish.

10 Sliced turkey and avocado with pepper jack cheese, melted. Or Turkey with mayo and chutney, cold.

WHEAT BERRY WHISKERS

2 T. wheat berries (find them at any food co-op or health store)

water

dirt

a clay flowerpot

Soak the berries overnight in water. Put dirt in the flowerpot and plant them. When the green spears appear, present the pot to your cat, or prepare a bunch of them for the next Humane Society flea market. Serves 1 cat.

Cats chew grass to extract the folic acid necessary for the production of hemoglobin.

THE CAT'S MEOW – A BASIC FOOD

2 cups water

2/3 cup rice

4 tsp. corn oil

1 tsp. salt (iodized)

1 1/3 cups raw meat, ground

4 T. raw liver, chopped

2 T. steamed bone meal (health or pet stores)

Bring the water to a boil in a good-sized saucepan, add the next 3 ingredients and simmer for 15 minutes. Meanwhile, mix the rest of the ingredients in a separate bowl, and when the 15 minutes are up, blend them into the saucepan and continue to simmer for another 15 minutes. Let the food cool and then divide it into 6 portions, freezing half of them (food for cats should never be kept for more than four days). Makes 6 servings.

You can use anything you like for meat, including poultry and fish. Rice can be brown or white, and potatoes or barley make an excellent replacement. Liver is a must. According to our vet, you can freeze it easily. Buy a pound or two of liver (beef is fine – it needn't be calf), grind or chop it, and simmer for 15 minutes. Drain it, saving the liquid for a later treat, and divide it into 16 or 32 parts, putting each one into an ice-cube compartment, ready for whenever you need a 1-oz. (or about 2 tsp.) portion.

Cats never strike a pose that isn't photogenic. Lillian Jackson Braun

FELINE FAST FOOD

2/3 cup cottage cheese

1/3 cup biscuit mix

2 T. chopped liver, cooked

2 T. corn oil

¼ tsp. salt

Combine all the ingredients and serve. This can be stored in a covered container in the refrigerator or frozen in individual portions. It's perfect when there's no time to cook. Serves 3.

Hair-ball alert: Prevent them by adding a teaspoon of mineral oil once a week to your cat's food; help eliminate them by putting a bit of Vaseline onto your cat's nose.

BEYOND MEOW MIX: FOR A CAT'S BIRTHDAY PARTY

4 cans sardines in oil, the 3¾-oz. size

1-1/3 cups cooked rice, cooled

2 T. chopped liver, cooked

½ cup fresh chives or parsley, chopped

pretzel sticks for candles

Combine all the ingredients in a bowl, crushing the sardines into the mix (include the oil), and divide it into 6 individual bowls for the honoree and the guests. Top with the pretzels, sing something, and serve. Serves 6.

A cat does not need water or food in its travel carrier. Cats can survive without water for 24 hours, and longer without food.

ANITRA FRAZIER'S VITA-MINERAL MIX

1½ cups yeast powder, nutritional or brewer's

½ cup kelp powder or granules

1 cup lecithin granules

1 cup wheat germ, toasted

1 cup bran

½ cup dolomite or bone meal

Combine all the ingredients and store them in a tightly covered container in the refrigerator. Put 2½ tsp. in each 6½-oz. can of cat food for that extra boost of vitamins and minerals.

Leftover shards of watermelon are a very refreshing addition to yogurt in the summer, especially sprinkled with lime juice.

H.S.K.C. CAT STEW

1 cup rice, preferably brown

2 cups broth or water

¼ lb. chicken livers or leftover meat cooked in broth, chopped

Cook the rice in the broth – it will yield 2 cups – and add the meat. If you have no liver or leftovers, use a can of cat food. Serve warm. This brew is cooked up often, usually in double batches, by the wonderful volunteers at the Humane Society of Knox County, when large colonies of kittens are in residence, or it's cold outside, or when the population of waifs and strays needs a pickup.

Flea powder can be applied to a pet without forming a mushroom cloud by using an old sock; put the powder in it and rub it gently on the animal, following the cautionary directions on the package.

NELLIE-THE-LIGHTHOUSE-DOG'S CHOCOLATE TREATS

2 T. corn oil or margarine

2 squares unsweetened chocolate

2 cups water or milk

3 T. brown sugar

3½ cups whole wheat flour

2½ cups oatmeal

Preheat the oven to 300. In a double boiler or heavy-bottomed pan, heat the first 4 ingredients until the chocolate melts. Combine the flour and the oatmeal in a good-sized bowl and stir in the chocolate mixture – it will be stiff. On a greased cookie sheet, pat the dough out to about ½" thick and bake it for 1 hour; it should be brown and crisp. Cut it into squares while it's still warm. (Chocolate in large doses is not good for dogs; if you don't want to use chocolate, substitute peanut butter.) Makes 5-6 dozen.

NELLIE'S RYE CRISPS

2 cups rye flour

¼ cup wheat flour

¼ cup corn meal

6 T. vegetable oil

2/3 cup warm water

Preheat the oven to 350. Combine the dry ingredients and then stir in the oil and the warm water. Form the mixture into a ball and then pat or roll it out to ¼" thick. Cut it into puppy-pleasing shapes and bake them on a greased cookie sheet for 30-40 minutes. Makes 24 canine crackers.

CHESTER'S CHOICE:
BIRTHDAY CAKE FOR GOOD DOGS

2/3 cup shortening

1 egg

1 tsp. brown sugar

1 cup milk

¼ cup A.1. sauce

1 T. Gravy Master

½ tsp. garlic powder

3 T. beef bouillon granules or equivalent cubes

2½ cups flour

Preheat the oven to 350. Combine the shortening, egg, and brown sugar. Add all the other ingredients except the flour and mix well, then stir in the flour in two or three batches. Pour it into a greased 8" cake pan and bake for 20-25 minutes. Decorate the cake with candles, sing, slice, and serve.

Outside of a dog, a book is man's best friend. Inside of a dog, it's too dark to read. Groucho Marx

BETSY'S DOG-BONE BISCUITS

1 cup all-purpose flour

1 cup wheat flour

½ cup wheat germ

½ cup non-fat dry milk

6 T. margarine

1 large egg

1 T. brown sugar

3 T. liver powder or veggie flakes

½ cup water

Preheat the oven to 325. Combine all the ingredients – the mixture will be quite stiff. Roll it out to about ¼" thick and cut it with a bone-shaped cookie cutter. Bake the biscuits for half an hour. Great for Christmas presents – pack them in a bag with a red ribbon! Makes about 3 dozen.

For flea prevention, sprinkle borax over carpets and floors and leave it for several hours before vacuuming. Do not try to remove all of it; what remains in floor cracks and rugs will discourage fleas. Also, all washing of floors should be done with Citra-solv, a natural based cleaner which actually uses citrus. "Green" stores and health food shops stock it.

RUMPOLE'S ROCKS: A DOGGONE GOOD SNACK

3 cups oatmeal

3½ cups whole wheat flour

½ cup powdered milk

½ cup bacon grease or leftover fat

2 eggs

2 tsp. cod-liver oil

1½ cups canned beef or chicken gravy

Preheat the oven to 325. Combine all the above ingredients and drop the mixture by spoonfuls onto an ungreased baking sheet. Bake for 50 minutes and cool the "rocks" on wire racks in a safe place. Store them in a covered container and distribute when behavior dictates. Makes 30.

Let us love dogs. Let us love only dogs. Men and cats are unworthy creatures. Marie Konstantinova Bashkirtseff

MARINER KENNELS WHOLE WHEAT DOG DELIGHTS

2½ cups whole wheat flour

¼ cup regular wheat germ

½ cup instant nonfat dry milk

½ tsp. garlic salt

6 T. corn oil margarine

1 egg, beaten

1 T. molasses

½ cup ice water

Preheat the oven to 375. Combine the dry ingredients. Cut in the margarine until the mixture resembles corn meal. Stir in the egg and molasses, and add enough ice water so that the mixture forms a ball. Roll the dough out on a floured board to a thickness of ¼", and cut it into shapes with a (bone-shaped) cookie cutter. Place them on a greased cookie sheet and bake for 20 minutes. Makes about 60.

To remove pet stains from hardwood floors: first try sponging with equal parts of household ammonia and water; let it dry. Next, clean the area with steel wool moistened with mineral spirits (paint thinner). Pour vinegar on the stain, let it work for several minutes, and brush it off with a stiff brush. Rinse the area and let it dry, repeating the process once or twice more if necessary. Finally, let the wood dry and lightly sand it with fine sandpaper, feathering the surrounding finish. Wax and polish. If the stain is still visible, try oxalic acid, following directions on the package.

CHASE'S CHEESE BONES

2 cups all-purpose flour

1¼ cups shredded cheese (your choice)

2 garlic cloves, minced

½ cup vegetable oil

¼ cup water (more or less)

Preheat the oven to 400. Combine the flour, cheese, garlic, and oil. Add water if necessary to form a stiff dough and knead well. Roll it out on a floured surface to ½" thick and cut it into shapes. Bake on an ungreased cookie sheet for 10-15 minutes, or until the bottoms are lightly browned. Makes about 3 dozen.

It is very important to handle and speak to puppies and kittens frequently between 2 and 7 weeks of age.

BUCKWHEAT'S CHRISTMAS BISCUITS

1 envelope yeast

¼ cup warm water (110-115 degrees)

3½ cups all-purpose flour

2 cups whole wheat flour

1 cup rye flour

2 cups cracked wheat

1 cup corn meal

½ cup instant non-fat dry milk

4 tsp. garlic salt

3-4 cups broth

1 egg beaten with 2 T. water for glaze

Preheat the oven to 300. Sprinkle yeast over warm water and stir to dissolve; reserve. In a very large bowl, combine the next 7 ingredients. Add 2 or 3 cups of broth and mix in the yeast. Work it with your hands to form a stiff dough, adding more broth if needed. Turn the dough onto a floured board and roll it to about ¼" thick. Cut it with a bone-shaped cookie cutter. Place the bones on an ungreased cookie sheet, brush them with the glaze, and bake for about 45 minutes. Cool the biscuits on a wire rack well out of a dog's reach. Let them harden overnight. Put a red bow around each one, and distribute them to your best friend's friends. Makes about 5 dozen.

When a dog threatens you or your dog, say "Go home" in a loud, firm voice. If it does not move, pick up a stone or a large stick. Sometimes even the gesture of bending down when no object is there is enough to send the dog away.

MAINE MASH FOR HORSES

7½ cups bran
3½ cups oats
4 cups carrots, sliced
enough hot water to cover

Combine all of the ingredients and let them sit for 5 minutes, covered, before serving. Makes 1 bucketful.

QUICKIE TOAST SNACK FOR PONIES

1 slice whole wheat bread
jam
sugar

Toast the bread and spread it with the jam and the sugar. Cut it into quarters and reward a loyal steed. Serves 1.

In the fall, for an extra treat, add 1 cup of pasteurized, non-fermented fresh apple cider to your horse's food.

MANE 'N' TAIL COCKTAIL TREATS

3 carrots, shredded

2 apples, chopped into small pieces

½ cup molasses

½ cup bran

6 Triscuits, chopped

other Triscuits for serving

Combine everything but the serving Triscuits, and chill overnight. Spread the stuff onto the serving Triscuits and hand them around in the barn at cocktail time. Serves about 6 .

Haunt yard sales and Goodwill for old afghans – they work as both cooler and sweat sheet combined, especially when the horse has been exercising heavily.

CREIGHTON'S CARROT BRAN CUPS

2 cups flour

½ cup sugar

2 cups bran

2 carrots, grated

1 T. soft margarine

1 tsp. baking powder

1 tsp. baking soda

Preheat the oven to 350. Grease 6 large muffin cups. Stir all of the ingredients together in a large bowl and divide it among the muffin cups. Bake them for 30 minutes, or until a toothpick comes out clean. Makes 6 horses happy.

You can bang a weighted, cleaned-out gallon bleach bottle from the ceiling of your horse's stall for a toy.

GRANOLA SURPRISE FOR THE GUYS IN THE BARN

  2 cups oatmeal

  1 cup bran

  ¼ cup sugar

  ¼ cup molasses

  2 T. honey

  ¼ cup water

Combine everything but the water and mix it well, adding the water until the gunk is thick but not runny. Refrigerate it for 1-2 hours, and form it into lumps the size of meatballs. Feed them to your horses. (Granola bars – the real thing – will do in an emergency.) Makes a dozen.

Save all of your old hairbrushes for grooming manes and tails, and your old toothbrushes for cleaning hooves. Hang onto those old, worn and torn sheets and towels, too; they're great for bandages and for drying off the animals.

THE BEER BRAN MASH

8 cups bran

8 cups oats

enough hot water to moisten

a bottle of beer or stout

Mix the bran and the oats together, adding enough hot water to moisten them. Let the stuff cool, and, just before serving, pour in the beer. Give it to a horse after heavy exercise. Makes a lot.

Use oversize blankets for horse coolers — heavy for winter, and lightweight for summer — and sew tapes on them for fastening. You'll save fifty dollars every time. Regular size blankets work for ponies.

ETCETERA

10 Gifts to Make from This Cookbook

1 Gifted Bread

2 Cracked Pepper Oil

3 Instant Gratification Microwave Chocolate Fix

4 Almond Crunch for the Host

5 Mrs. Jaquinto's Winter Sachet – A Mothball Substitute

6 Seafood Pepper-Spice Mix to Use in Your Extra Pepper Grinder

7 Nuts to You, Microwave

8 For the Kids: Bubble Liquid

9 Whole Wheat Beer Bread in a Clay Flowerpot

10 Papo's Tasty Turtles

GIFTED BREAD

1 recipe for your favorite bread
1 yard 1½" gift ribbon

Make the bread in the usual way until after the first rise, when you have punched it down and rested it for 15 minutes, in a covered bowl. It should now be shaped into a rectangle, 5x8, on a floured surface. From a large brown paper grocery bag, cut 2 strips 1½" wide – one 20" long, the other 15" long. Place them on a greased baking sheet, crossed. Brush them with melted butter. Place the bread in the center over the strips, and brush it with melted butter. Loosely wrap the strips around the bread, trimming them and fastening with tooth picks or paper clips. There should be room for a finger under each one. Let the bread rise until it's double in size, about an hour, and bake as usual. When you remove it from the baking sheet, take off the paper strips and cool it on a wire rack. You'll know what to do with the gift ribbon.

SPEEDY LEMON PEPPER BREADSTICKS

½ tsp. lemon peel, minced (lemon zest)
1 T. lemon juice
1 T. water
¼ tsp. salt
½ tsp. cracked pepper
1 pkg. refrigerated or heat-and-serve breadsticks

Preheat the oven according to the package, and combine all the ingredients except the breadsticks. Arrange them on an ungreased cookie sheet, and, if refrigerated, twist the ends in opposite directions several times. Brush the sticks with the lemon pepper mixture and bake until browned, using the package instructions. Makes 8 sticks.

COFFEE CAN OLIVE BREAD

2 cups all-purpose flour

2 tsp. baking powder

2 T. sugar or honey

½ cup milk

2 large eggs, beaten

1½ cups olives, any kind, drained and rough chopped

2 T. olive oil

optional: ½ tsp. hot pepper flakes or onion flakes

Preheat the oven to 350, and oil a coffee can (or a 4x8 loaf pan). In a large bowl, combine the first 3 ingredients and stir in the milk. In another, combine the rest of the ingredients. Add this to the first bowl, mix, and pour the batter into the coffee can. Bake it for 1 hour, or until a toothpick comes out clean. Allow the bread to cool for 10 minutes before turning it onto a rack. (A sun-dried tomato buff substituted ¾ cup of them for olives, the other half consisting of Greek olives, and was very enthusiastic about the results.) Makes 1 loaf.

Of course one can bake the bread in a loaf pan, but it's so easy to put together, a child can do it, and the coffee can idea might just tempt a fledgling cook.

A 10-year-old child is old enough to take over a pet's feeding and exercise, but a 3 or 4-year-old can only love it and play with it.

WHOLE WHEAT BEER BREAD

3 cups whole wheat flour

1 tsp. baking powder

½ tsp. baking soda

¼ cup honey or molasses

1 12-oz. bottle of dark beer

Preheat oven to 350. Combine the dry ingredients. Stir in the honey, add the beer, and mix only until everything is moistened. Bake 55-60 minutes in a greased loaf pan which has been sprinkled with corn meal. If you want a glaze, during the last 10 minutes of baking brush the top with a bit of lightly beaten eggbeater or egg white mixed with 2 T. cold water. You can also sprinkle the top with bacon bits, crushed cereal, oatmeal, etc. This bread makes great sandwiches, and gives the term PB&J a whole new meaning. Makes 1 loaf.

Have you ever baked bread in a clay flowerpot? It used to be done in France, and works like a charm — just make or buy your favorite dough, and bake it in a well-buttered pot (we used a 6" one), making sure to cover the hole in the bottom with a clean penny or a piece of foil. Needless to say, the kids love it, and they can help.

MAKE A FOCACCIA, IT'S A SNAP WITH A PROCESSER

1 pkg. yeast in 1 cup warm water (about 110 degrees)

3 cups flour

1 tsp. salt

2 T. olive oil

olive oil, coarse salt, fresh rosemary, Greek olives, etc. for
toppings

Mix the yeast and warm water in a small bowl and let it sit while you prepare the rest: put the flour, salt, and olive oil into the bowl of the processer and process briefly to mix it, about 10 seconds. Then add the yeast water slowly until the dough forms a ball. Put it into an oiled bowl, turning to coat, cover it with plastic wrap, and let it rise to double its size – for about an hour. Then punch it down and let it rest for 10 minutes before rolling and shaping. Prepare a greased baking sheet or a 12" pizza pan. Roll the dough out to the shape you want (it will be about 12"x18" and ½" thick on a baking sheet, and thicker in a 12" pizza pan) and put it into the pan. Dimple the entire surface of the dough with your fingertips (as the bakers of Genoa do to trap the oil and salt that flavor the bread). Cover it and let it rise again, for 20 minutes. Meanwhile, preheat the oven to 425. Brush the focaccia with olive oil and top it with whatever you like, ending with a sprinkle of salt – fresh rosemary and garlic slivers, or Greek olives placed around the edge with slivered garlic, for instance. You'll soon make up your own combinations. Bake it for 25 minutes or until it sounds hollow when you tap it. Serves 8-10.

How about trying it on the grill? A gas grill is easiest, because the heat can be controlled, but don't be afraid to experiment with charcoal. After it has rested for 20 minutes on a baking sheet, place the sheet on the grill at medium heat and bake it for 2 minutes, to stiffen it. Turn the grill on low (or use the part away from the direct heat) and transfer the bread from the sheet to the grill, baking it for another 6 or 7 minutes, watching it like a hawk, until the bottom is slightly charred and the bread is crusty.

SMALL WONDERS: IMPROMPTU PIZZAS

1 tsp. sugar

2 cups warm water

2 packages active dry yeast

1 tsp. salt

4 cups flour

2 T. olive oil, plus more for drizzling

3-4 small fresh tomatoes, sliced thin

salt and pepper

6 T. mozzarella, sliced thin

2-3 cloves garlic, slivered

8 leaves fresh basil, snipped

In a large bowl, dissolve the sugar in the water, and then whisk in the yeast. Cover it with plastic wrap and let it rest for 20 minutes. Meanwhile, mix the salt and flour in a separate bowl and prepare the topping, whatever it may be (in this case, fresh sliced tomato and mozzarella cheese with garlic and basil). Preheat the oven to 450, and spray or oil 3 cookie sheets. Uncover the bowl, add the olive oil, and whisk in about 2/3 of the flour. Stir in the rest with a wooden spoon – don't worry if the dough is soft. With a large metal spoon, plop 8-10 portions of dough onto the cookie sheets. Dip your fingers into the olive oil, and quickly flatten them into informal circles. Top them with your chosen ingredients, drizzling with oil at the end, if you wish. Bake them for about 20 minutes, until the crust is crisp. Makes 8-10.

Everyone loves to get into the act when these leftover-loving, fast-cooking pizzas are made, especially the kids. For a supper with salad, or for hot or cold appetizers (cut into wedges), they are perfect. Try any sort of pesto or salsa as a base, with whatever you like on top; celebrate with split raw shrimp (added for the last 5 minutes) or smoked mussels; find a surprise in the refrigerator – this fodder is sheer fun.

A dog's nose in the palm of your hand can cure anything.

FOUR CROWNS FOR A STEW:

HERB DUMPLINGS

  2 cups biscuit mix

  2/3 cup cold milk, broth, or water

  1 T. fresh parsley, chopped

  1 T. any other herb or herbs, fresh or dry, in any combination

Combine everything in a bowl; drop by spoonfuls onto a boiling stew or soup. Cover tightly, reduce heat, and simmer for 12-15 minutes.

CHEESE AND PEPPER CRATERS

  2 cups biscuit mix

  2/3 cup cold milk, broth, or water

  1 cup very sharp cheese, grated

  1 T. coarsely ground black pepper

Combine everything in a bowl. Using two spoons, or a couple of well-floured hands, scatter in lumps (like the surface of the moon) onto a boiling stew or soup, cover tightly, reduce heat and simmer for 12-15 minutes.

A dog is a dog, a bird is a bird, and a cat is a person.
Mugsy Peabody

TEXAS CORN MEAL TOPPING

1 pkg. (8 ½-oz.) corn muffin mix

¾ cup milk, broth, or water

½ cup cheddar or pepper jack cheese, shredded,

½ cup canned corn: creamed or regular

1 jalapeño pepper, seeded and minced

Combine everything in a bowl; it should be loose and lumpy. Drop by spoonfuls onto a boiling stew or soup, cover tightly, reduce heat, and simmer for 12-15 minutes.

PARSLEY-ONION ROLL-UPS

1 cup biscuit mix

1/3 cup milk, broth, or water

1 onion, finely chopped and sautéed in butter

¼ cup fresh parsley, minced

In a bowl, combine the biscuit mix and the liquid and beat it for 15 strokes. Turn it onto a floured board, and roll it out to a rectangle, about ¼" thick. Spread the onions over the dough, sprinkle it with the parsley and roll it up from the wide side. Moisten the edges to seal. Cut the roll into about 10 slices and place them on top of any boiling stew or soup. Cover the pot, reduce the heat, and simmer for 12-15 minutes.

Four legs good, two legs bad. George Orwell

SUPERMARKET MUFFULETTA FOR THE BOAT

1 round loaf of bread, about 1 lb.

olive oil and vinegar for sprinkling; ditto salt and pepper

½ lb. supermarket salad bar Italian relish (the one with the olives, peppers, cheese, and salami cubes, etc.), chopped coarsely

½-¾ lb. sliced turkey breast

2 tomatoes, sliced

½ cucumber, peeled and sliced

optional: thin slices of Vidalia or red onion

The day before: slit the bread in half and remove the innards, leaving a ½" shell, more or less, and begin building. Sprinkle the insides of the shells liberally with the vinegar, oil, salt and pepper. Now divide the relish in half and slather it onto each shell. Add, until they are used up, slices of turkey, cucumber, and tomato, sprinkling with salt and pepper when needed. Any personal touches you wish to include, from leftovers to naughty delights like thin slices of Genoa salami and provolone cheese, are fair game; just create and enjoy. The halves are then pressed together and put into a plastic bag, very tightly fastened with a twist tie, and placed in the refrigerator with a weight on top, there to remain until serving time, when the loaf is sliced into wedges and enjoyed with lots of orange soda and root beer. Serves 4-6.

Naughty is neater: the salami and cheese stick together and make a tighter sandwich, but healthy tomatoes and cukes, though they tend to cause "sliding" are really the way to go. This is your mother speaking.

When man is lonely, God sends him a dog. Lamartine

TRUE'S OVERNIGHT MERINGUES FOR WHEN YOUR CHILD ANNOUNCES AT 11:00PM THAT SHE HAS TO BRING SOMETHING TO SCHOOL IN THE MORNING

2 egg whites
pinch of salt
2/3 cup sugar
½ tsp. vanilla

Preheat the oven to 375. Beat the whites with the salt until stiff. Slowly add the sugar and then the vanilla, still beating, until everything has been absorbed. Drop the mixture by teaspoons onto greased cookie sheets. Put them into the preheated oven, close the oven door, TURN THE OVEN OFF, and go to bed. When you wake up the next morning, remove the meringues from the trays, put them into a cookie tin, and hand it to your child. You'll have made about 2 dozen.

Optional fold-ins: 6 oz. chocolate bits, chopped nuts, red hots (for Valentine's Day)

The cryptics name their dogs October, Bennett's Aunt, Three Fifteen, Doc Knows, Tuesday, Home Fried, Opus 38, Ask Leslie, and Walter S. Bursley. I make it a point simply to pat these unfortunate dogs on the head, ask no questions, and go about my business.
James Thurber

PAPO'S TASTY TURTLES

1 ¼ cups milk chocolate or semi-sweet chocolate bits

1 T. water or coffee

4 T. light corn syrup

1 ½ cups pecans, almonds, etc., or combo, toasted

optional: ½ tsp. instant espresso powder

Line 2 baking sheets with wax paper. Combine everything but the nuts in the top of a double boiler and heat over gently simmering water, stirring until the chocolate is melted. Remove from the heat, stir in the nuts, drop by spoonfuls onto the baking sheet and chill until the chocolate hardens. Makes 24 .

A handy chocolate-decorating tube can be made with one of those extra-strong plastic zip-top bags: put some chopped-up chocolate (any color – pale, white, dark) in the bag, partially seal it, and let it sit in a bowl of hot water with the top sticking out until the chocolate melts. Dry it off, snip off a tiny bit of one corner, and begin. Contrasting shades of chocolate – pale or white on dark – are very effective.

One of the ways cats show happiness is by sleeping.
Cleveland Amory

ALMOND CRUNCH FOR THE HOST

1 cup slivered or sliced almonds, toasted

2/3 cup butter

1 cup sugar

6 oz. chocolate: ¾ cup semi-sweet bits, 2 squares unsweetened, chopped

Prepare an 8x8 pan by lining it with aluminum foil, lightly oiled. Reserve ¼ cup of the nuts, and chop them finely. Combine the butter and sugar in a saucepan over low heat, stirring until the sugar melts. Add the rest of the nuts and cook the mixture to 290 on a candy thermometer (crack stage), stirring occasionally. Pour it into the prepared pan and distribute the chocolate evenly over the top. Let it soften for a few minutes, and then spread it with a rubber spatula and sprinkle with the reserved nuts. Cool and then refrigerate until it's hard. Remove the slab from the pan, and break it into pieces. Wrap them in a nice package, and apologize for the broken wine glass. Makes about 1 lb.

An old wooden lobster pot marker (the kind that looks like a buoy) hanging in a horse's stall makes a nice toy for him to play with.

INSTANT GRATIFICATION
MICROWAVE CHOCOLATE FIX

1 cup whole almonds, toasted

12 oz. chocolate, your choice, chopped

Almonds can be toasted in the microwave on a paper plate or towel on HIGH for 2 minutes. Check them, stir, and try another 30 seconds, stirring each time, until ready. They should stand for 5 minutes. Or you can do them in the toaster oven at 325 for 10-15 minutes, watching carefully for doneness. Meanwhile, line the bottom of a 9x13 baking pan with a double thickness of wax paper, and scatter the almonds evenly on it. Arrange the chocolate (we used 1½ cups chocolate bits and 3 squares of unsweetened, chopped) around the edge of a glass pie plate (be sure it is completely dry), leaving a space in the center, and cook on HIGH for 2 minutes. Stir to see that it is completely melted, and if not, give it another 30 seconds, no more – you do not want to scorch it. Pour the chocolate over the nuts, smoothing it to cover them evenly, and chill it in the refrigerator until hard. (If you are really in a hurry, use the freezer – five minutes, tops.)   Break the candy into pieces and pass it around. Satisfies 1-6.

Make chocolate birds' nests by melting a 12-oz. package of chocolate bits in a double boiler with ½ cup chunky peanut butter, and adding 10-12 finely crushed shredded wheat biscuits to it. Drop by spoonfuls onto wax paper, press them into nest shapes with a spoon, and chill. Put a few jelly beans or speckled egg candies in each one.

1½ cups nuts, e.g. almonds
1 tsp. oil
1 tsp. liquid smoke or hickory salt
salt to taste

1 cup nuts, e.g. peanuts
1 tsp. oil
1 T. honeycup mustard

1 1/3 cup nuts, e.g. pecans
1 tsp. oil
few drops Chinese hot-and-spicy oil
1 tsp. powdered chilis, ¼ tsp. at a time
¼ tsp. Tabasco, or to taste
salt to taste

The rule is: nuts go into a glass pie plate, oil is added and stirred to coat them, and then the spices and flavorings are mixed in. The nuts are toasted on HIGH for 3-5 minutes and stirred every 2 minutes. After that, they are toasted in 30-second intervals, stirred each time to redistribute the heat, and removed when lightly toasted, to rest for 5-10 minutes while they finish "cooking". A cup of nuts should take about 2-5 minutes. More nuts take more time, in case you double or triple the recipe. As for the last version, for dedicated chili pepper fans everywhere, do NOT put all the powdered chilis in at once: after the 2-minute stir, taste for heat, and add more if you dare.

Have a toast-off, and make up your own combinations: Chinese dipping sauce, satay sauce, Cajun blackened seasoning rub; whatever you can dream up. Award the winner a visit to Perry's Nut House, on Route 1 just east of Belfast where, it is said, Eleanor Roosevelt used to stop on her way to Campobello.

GRANDMA OLIVE'S LEGENDARY CARAMELS

2 cups sugar

1 ½ cups light corn syrup

2 cups cream (1 cup half-and-half; 1 cup heavy)

½ cup butter (1 stick)

1 tsp. vanilla

½ cup toasted nuts (any kind)

Butter an 8x8 square baking pan – either glass or metal. Mix the sugar and the corn syrup in a heavy 3-quart saucepan; bring it to a boil. Add the cream VERY SLOWLY. Add the butter. Cook, slowly, to 245 on a candy thermometer (in summer, 248). Add the vanilla and the nuts and pour the candy into the buttered pan. When it's cool, cut it into small square pieces and wrap them in wax paper. This is a luxurious gift of love. Makes about 100.

Someday try substituting 2 T. of rum for the vanilla; it's not Grandma Olive, but it's not bad either.

Scientists have identified three personality types in cats: sociable and confident; timid, shy, and unfriendly; and active and aggressive.

POTATO MOUNDS BARS
FROM DAWN'S GRANDMOTHER

1 medium Maine potato (½ cup), peeled, boiled, and mashed

1 T. butter

1 tsp. vanilla

1 lb. powdered sugar

¼ tsp. salt

1 cup shredded coconut

2 squares bittersweet chocolate, melted

Combine all the ingredients except the chocolate, blending well. Add more sugar or coconut if you want it thicker. Pack it evenly into a well-buttered 8x8 square pan (which you may also line with buttered wax paper), and spread the top with the melted chocolate. Let it cool or refrigerate it before cutting into small rectangles. Makes 24 small bars.

FOR THE KIDS: BUBBLE LIQUID

¼ cup hot water

2 tsp. sugar

1/3 cup liquid dish soap or baby shampoo

Dissolve the sugar in the water, then add the soap. Some dish soaps have a lovely color; using shampoo prevents stinging bubbles in the eyes. Make your own wands by bending thin metal wire, if there's some in the tool box. Enjoy!

Start kittens early with human toenail clippers; reward them afterwards.

CHRISTMAS PRESENT PEPPER JELLY

2 fresh bell peppers: red or green, trimmed, seeded, and rough
    chopped

4-6 fresh jalapeño chilis

1 ½ cups cider or plain vinegar

6 cups sugar

6 oz. liquid pectin (2 3-oz. pouches)

optional: red or green food coloring

Choose one color, red or green, for each batch. Puree the peppers with the vinegar (in batches if necessary) until they are small enough for your jelly. Mix them with the sugar in a large saucepan and bring to a boil. Simmer for 10 minutes. Add the pectin, stir, and boil for 1 minute more. Remove from the heat, skim foam from the top, add food coloring if you wish, stir, and let stand for 10-15 minutes. Pour the jelly into sterile jars and seal with paraffin. Give pairs of jars as gifts: one red, one green. Makes about 4 cups.

The best protection against street crime is a big dog that scares people on sight.

MAINE BLUEBERRY PRESERVES WITH CURAÇAO

5 cups wild Maine blueberries

3 cups sugar

¼-½ cup curaçao or orange-flavored liqueur

Wash the berries and put them in a large pot with the sugar. Cook over low heat until the sugar melts. Add the curaçao and gently simmer for 20-30 minutes until it reaches the soft-ball stage (240 degrees). Pour it into hot, sterile, 8-oz. jelly glasses and top with paraffin at once. Cool them before covering with lids. Makes 4 or 5 8-oz. jars.

LIME JELLY WITH FRESH MINT

2 dozen limes: their juice and zest

4 cups sugar

1-1/3 cups limeade or water

2 cups fresh mint leaves, chopped

In a large saucepan, cook everything but the mint until it reaches 220 on a thermometer, or the soft-ball stage (when the jelly falls from the spoon in one drop, not two). Take it off the stove, stir in the mint leaves, and pour the jelly into sterilized jars. Seal them and process for 5 minutes, or else cool and seal with paraffin. Makes 4 half-pint jars.

Make this in the summer, when limes are plentiful and cheap, and there's plenty of fresh mint around.

In a cat's eyes, all things belong to cats. English proverb

AUNTIE RUTH'S WAY HOT CHILI SAUCE

1 peck tomatoes (8 qts.), scalded, skinned, and chopped

1 big bunch celery – about 1 pound, chopped

1 qt. onions, or 3 good big ones, chopped

3 medium sweet green peppers, or 2 big ones, chopped

1 qt. cider vinegar

2 lb. brown sugar

¼ cup salt

1 T. dry mustard

½ T. ground cloves

1 tsp. ground cinnamon

salt to taste, if necessary

Tabasco or hot pepper sauce

Cook the tomatoes over medium heat for 15 minutes in a large enamel kettle. Add the next 9 ingredients and boil until thick, 2-3 hours, stirring frequently. Taste for salt, and if you are serious about hot, start adding hot sauce until you are happy. Ladle the sauce into sterile jars and seal. They do not need processing. Makes about 8 pints.

If you have hot peppers in your garden, by all means, use them instead of Tabasco, being careful to taste as you go. It goes without saying that one can leave out the heat altogether; this is a fabulous chili sauce, and well worth your time.

Never ask a hungry cat if he loves you for yourself alone.
Dr. Louis Camuti

GARLIC CONFIT BOB DAVIS: EASY ROASTED GARLIC

1 cup garlic cloves, peeled
enough olive oil to cover, about 1 cup

Simmer the above in a tiny saucepan, covered, for 20-25 minutes. Cool. Store them in a covered jar in the refrigerator (garlic in oil must always be refrigerated, or botulism can form in the oil), and use them sliced, for pizza toppings, spread on crusty bread, or for a special gift. The oil can be re-used, or serve as a delicious dip for bread. Makes 1 cup.

CRACKED PEPPER OIL

1 cup luxurious olive oil
2 T. black peppercorns

Crush the peppercorns by putting them between layers of a dish towel, or in a tough plastic bag, and rapping them with a heavy object, like the bottom of a skillet. Put them with the oil in a small saucepan, bring it to a boil, reduce the heat, and simmer for 10 minutes. Cool for 30 minutes to allow the flavor to infuse the oil as it cools. Pour it into a sterile bottle that can be corked, and keep it in the refrigerator. Nice for dipping bread; better for you than butter! Also fun to add to scrambled eggbeater omelets, or to paint on food for the grill, or to try in the next batch of cornbread. Makes 1 cup.

The cat is, above all, a dramatist. Margaret Benson

MRS. JAQUINTO'S WINTER SACHET:
A MOTHBALL SUBSTITUTE

½ lb. dry rosemary

¼ lb. dry thyme

½ lb. dry mint

2 T. cloves, crushed, or cinnamon stick, crushed

Mix all of it together well, seal the heavenly stuff in a plastic bag, and age it in the refrigerator for a week. Tie portions of it into cotton or linen squares with ribbon and tuck the sachets into pockets or folds of coats, sweaters, furs, and woolens as moth repellents.

SEAFOOD PEPPER-SPICE MIX
TO USE IN YOUR EXTRA PEPPER GRINDER

1 T. black peppercorns

1 T. white or green peppercorns

1 tsp. coriander seeds

1 tsp. fennel seeds

1 tsp. celery seeds

1 tsp. hot red pepper flakes

Mix the above ingredients in a small cup and pour the batch into your grinder. (Should you have time, the corns and seeds will intensify in flavor if you heat them in a small skillet – shaking them for a few minutes until they begin to "dance" – before putting them into the grinder.) Use the mix on seafood and in salads.

Both of these would make great gifts – the sachet with the sweater you finished just in time; and the pepper in a new Lucite grinder for your piano teacher.

CHAMPAGNE JELLY WITH ROSE PETALS

juice of 1 lemon and some of its peel

1 cup water

1 envelope unflavored gelatin

2 T. sugar

1 cup champagne

a few fragrant rose petals, cut into small pieces – about 1 T.

Mix the lemon juice with ¼ cup of the water in a small vessel, and add the gelatin to soften while you prepare the rest of the dish. With a vegetable peeler, cut 8 strips of lemon peel and put them in a small sauce pan with the rest of the water and the sugar. Add the gelatin mix and heat to just below the boiling point. Remove it from the stove, cover it, and let it cool for about 20 minutes. Strain the liquid into a bowl and chill it almost to the setting point, about an hour. Prepare the rose petals and stir them in, and then add the champagne, very gently, so as not to lose the bubbles. Spoon it into clear stemmed glasses or thin glass cups and refrigerate until set. Don't make it too far ahead, or the dessert will lose its fizz. Serve, if you like, with cut-up fresh fruit in sugar and cognac. These jellies can also go to a picnic, poured into small clear molds, also accompanied by fruit. Serves 4-6.

For a big bash, consider using scraps of gold leaf (yes, it is edible in small amounts) and tying gold ribbons on the goblets.

For crystal clear iced tea, make it the day before by putting 12 tea bags in a gallon of cold water and refrigerating it overnight.

"ROBERT'S OPENING" CHAMPAGNE PUNCH

1 decorated ice ring for garnish

1 qt. prepared limeade for ice ring

1 lemon, sliced

2 limes, sliced

1 cup white wine

½ cup sugar

½ cup brandy

2 cups white wine, chilled

2 bottles champagne, chilled

For the ice ring, use a ring mold and gather fresh rose buds or blossoms, or sprigs of mint, or strawberries, etc. Pour the limeade into the mold in thin layers over the chosen decorations to anchor them. Do this at least a day ahead of time. For the punch, mash and macerate for 1 hour the next five ingredients and chill. When you are ready to serve, pour them into a bowl with the rest of the ingredients and add the ice ring. Serves 10-20.

A lame cat is better than a swift horse when rats infest the palace.
Chinese proverb

TEQUILA MOCKINGBIRD: A CEREMONIAL DRINK

1 3-oz. pkg. lime Jell-O

½ cup fresh lime juice (3 limes) pulp included

1 cup limeade prepared from frozen concentrate

¾ cup tequila

20 3-oz. plastic cups

optional: green Tabasco sauce

In a small container, empty the Jell-O packet into the lime juice to soften. Meanwhile, heat the limeade (which you have made stronger than usual by adding about 1/3 less water than the directions call for) in a saucepan, so that the gelatin will dissolve. Stir the Jell-O mix into the saucepan, blend, and put the hot liquid in its pan into the refrigerator to chill. Keep your eye on it, and when it becomes cool, in about 45 minutes, add the tequila, blend, and put 2 T. of the liquid in each of 18-20 cups. Chill until wiggle-firm. For serving, put a bowl with 1" of hot water in it on a warmer. The drinker dips his cup briefly into the hot water to loosen the stuff, pops it into his mouth, and usually yelps. The brave (or foolish) will add a jolt of green Tabasco before gulping. These mockers are also portable: just warm them with your hands before quaffing. Makes about 20.

If shrimp happen to be on sale this week, think about marinating them, shelled or not, in a mixture of 2 parts limeade concentrate and 1 part tequila; and then grilling or broiling them. Your guests will dance all the way home.

GINGER SYRUP – A SUMMER DRINK TREAT

1 cup sugar

1 ½ cups water

½ cup ginger root, sliced

zest and juice of 1 lemon

In a small saucepan over low heat, dissolve the sugar in the water. Meanwhile, crush the ginger and add it with the lemon zest to the pan. Heat the syrup slowly to the boiling point, stirring, and boil for 5 minutes. Remove it from the stove, cover, and cool. When it is cool, strain it, discard the lemon zest and the ginger, and add the lemon juice. Store the syrup in a covered jar; to make a drink, mix 2 or 3 tablespoons with a cup of soda or water. Add ice and garnish with lemon, ginger or mint. Makes 2 cups.

WINDEX

1 tsp. blue curacao

2 oz. vodka

soda to taste

Put the first 2 ingredients in a stemmed glass, add ice, and fill with the soda. Serves 1. (In an unnamed school, in an unnamed closet, there's a Windex bottle which doesn't contain Windex.)

To make Tabasco ice cubes for Bloody Marys, combine 1 cup tomato juice, 2 T. lemon juice, 1 T. Worcestershire sauce, and 1 tsp. Tabasco, and freeze it overnight in an ice cube tray.

SANGRITA: A MEXICAN BLOODY MARY

2 cups tomato juice

1 cup orange juice

juice of 3 limes

2 T. grenadine or ¼ cup cranberry juice

a dash of Tabasco or chili pequin, or cayenne pepper

salt to taste

tequila

Combine everything but the tequila in a pitcher, tasting for the heat you want. Serve, a jigger at a time, followed by a jigger of tequila, or else serve by the ½ cupful with a jigger of tequila in a glass over ice. Makes 8 servings.

One year, a Christmas dinner guest arrived lugging bags of limes and an electric juicer, and proceeded to grind away with his loot until he produced enough of this fabulous drink for all. It's a huge favorite.

SANGRITA SORBET

2 fresh jalapeño peppers, seeded and cut up

2 cups tomatoes, peeled and chopped

juice of 3 limes

juice of 2 oranges

3 T. sugar

1/3 cup tequila

lime wedges for garnish

Puree everything in a processer or blender. Chill, and freeze it in an ice cream maker according to the manufacturer's directions. Serve it in stemmed glasses (whose rims have been dipped in lime juice and then salt?) and garnish with fresh lime wedges. Serves 6.

The cat is never vulgar. Carl Van Vechten

MILLY'S MANGO FANDANGO VINEGAR

    1 cup cider vinegar

    ¼ cup honey or sugar

    2 tsp. vanilla

    1 cup very ripe mango, peeled, seeded, cut up and pureed

Put the vinegar with the honey or sugar in a saucepan, and heat, stirring, just until the sugar is dissolved. When it is cool, combine it with the rest of the ingredients, and bottle it. Keep it in the refrigerator to use on leftover chicken or pork, grilled or broiled vegetables or meats, on greens, coleslaw, salads – and of course, on prosciutto and melon. Makes 1 pint.

Vinegars are fun and easy to make; all you need is imagination. A friend brought over a tropical spicy table vinegar which he uses as a dip for just about everything – it has ¼ tsp. coarse salt, 3 tsp. hot pepper flakes (or 4 dried chilis), 2 large cloves of garlic, halved, 1 tsp. whole peppercorns, and 3 nickel-sized slices of fresh ginger in 1 cup of clear vinegar. He bottles it and corks it, and renews the vinegar when it gets low. It can be used in salads, when you want heat. And when he uses it as a dip, he sometimes adds a bit of lime juice or soy sauce to it.

INDEX

252

The Humane Society of Knox County shelter was opened in November, 1991. Since that day over 1,300 animals have been adopted. Dogs and cats who have been abused, lost or abandoned have first priority. Kittens and puppies are fostered in private homes until they are eight weeks old. All animals are tested, treated, inoculated, bathed and spayed or neutered before they leave.

Representatives from other shelters have traveled from all parts of the country to study and take back ideas from this small rural sanctuary. A unique feature of this shelter in the woods, for instance, is a cat community porch where fresh air and the social interaction of animals and volunteers of all ages make H.S.K.C. cats user-friendly and good candidates for multiple child and animal homes.

A creative executive director, a dedicated staff of three, and many enthusiastic volunteers from the local and summer communities find inspiration and reward in the everyday miracle that unites a once scruffy frightened refugee with a loving companion and a permanent home.

Support comes from memberships, memorial donations, personal gifts, fund raising events, and projects like WORD OF MOUTH. If you, too, wish to share in this worthy endeavor, kindly consider your local (or our Maine H.S.K.C.) shelter, and fill out the form below.

- -

Having read WORD OF MOUTH, I would like to support homeless animals

Name_____

Address_____

Amount_____

Send a donation to your local animal shelter, or to the Humane Society of Knox County, P.O. Box 1294, Rockland, ME. 04841

- -

To order more books, send $14.95 plus $2.50 postage/handling to:

WORD OF MOUTH, Box 21, Tenants Harbor, ME., 04860

Name_____

Address_____